INSTR~~~~~ MANUAL FOR FORD TRIMOTOR AIRPLANE

by Stout Metal Aircraft Co.

-1929-

©2013 Periscope Film LLC
All Rights Reserved
ISBN#978-1-937684-53-2
www.PeriscopeFilm.com

INTRODUCTION

This book of service instructions and operating suggestions is offered for the guidance of owners, pilots and mechanics of Ford all-metal monoplanes. With the engine instruction book as a supplement, it is designed to thoroughly familiarize the operator with the plane.

Information contained in this volume is the result of study and observation of the tri-motor Ford monoplane under a variety of operating conditions, not only on commercial lines, but in private service as well. It represents the experience of both pilots and mechanics. Much space is devoted to structural details of the plane. Additional emphasis is laid on the personal element in flying.

The service obtained from an airplane is measured largely by the intelligence with which the plane is handled. Operators, pilots and mechanics should give this volume careful study immediately after delivery of a new plane. It should be remembered that the Ford monoplane is a substantial investment and should be treated as such. Regular inspection and service is the secret of lower upkeep costs and reduced depreciation charges.

In the interest of safety and regularity of operation of the plane, we recommend that pilots be requested to study in detail the section of this book entitled "Suggestions on the Operation of the Ford Tri-motor."

Figure 1—Ford Tri-Motor Monoplane equipped with Pontoons

Figure 2—Ford Tri-Motor Monoplane equipped with Skiis

Part I

GENERAL INFORMATION

*Suggestions on the Operation
of the Ford Tri-Motor*

General Description

Specifications—Equipment

SUGGESTIONS ON THE OPERATION OF THE FORD TRI-MOTOR

While it would be impossible to incorporate in a book of this kind full instructions covering the rules of safety for the operation of an airplane, the following suggestions if carefully studied will prove valuable.

Must Know Air Traffic Rules

All transport pilots are required by law to thoroughly familiarize them-selves with the "Air Traffic Rules" of the Department of Commerce, and with the regulations covering the operation and inspection of aircraft.

Do Not Overload Plane

The Department of Commerce license card in each airplane states the allowable gross load of that airplane. Operating the plane with a greater load than specified by the Department of Commerce is not only an infraction of the law, but a disregard of the rules of safety.

Overloading the tri-motor airplane not only increases its landing speed and the space necessary for taking off, but it destroys its otherwise excellent two engine performance. It is important that the load be evenly distributed in the cabin. Placing too much load in the rear of the cabin causes the plane to feel "loggy" in responding to the controls.

Taking Off

One of the important points to bear in mind when taking off a tri-motor airplane is that it is absolutely essential that all three engines are turning up steadily at full throttle. The importance of this cannot be over-emphasized. After checking position of gasoline control valves, each engine should be "run up" in turn before the ship is taken off. Sometimes, when all three engines are opened up for the take off, one engine, if the weather is cold, may miss and backfire. It is not as simple to detect this as one might suppose, as it is sometimes difficult to hear the missing engine above the noise of the other two. It is also difficult to glance at all three tachometers in a short interval of time. It is a good plan to open up the throttles on the two outboard engines to approximately 1000 R.P.M. before opening throttle for center engine.

If the ship is under way for the take off, and one engine cuts out momen-tarily, the only safe thing to do is to *shut off the other two engines,* and start the take off over again. An outboard engine failing when starting on the take off is apt to dangerously swerve the ship and, due to the low air speed, the rudder will not be powerful enough to correct it. If the engines show a tendency to cut out when the throttles are opened, the safest course to follow is to hold the brakes until all three engines are turning up satis-factorily. In any case, THE THROTTLES SHOULD BE OPENED SLOWLY. Make certain that the throttle adjusting nut is sufficiently tight to prevent any possibility of the throttle slipping back.

Before taking off, all engines should be opened to full throttle for a few seconds, but do not, under any circumstances, hold an air-cooled engine at full throttle on the ground any longer than is necessary to make sure it is operating satisfactorily. When the engine is "run up," the magneto switch should be turned to the "left" and "right" positions to determine whether both magnetos and all spark plugs are properly functioning.

It is extremely bad practice to open the throttles for a take off while the ship is rolling rapidly from a previous landing. Should an outboard engine fail under these circumstances, the ship would swerve sharply and be very difficult to control.

Before taking off, the pilot should be certain that he knows approximately where the stabilizer is set. The airplane will take off, and have adequate longitudinal control for both positive and negative pitch, with any stabilizer setting, however if the stabilizer is set at extreme angles the forces required to operate the elevators are exceptionally great.

The control wheel is marked with the "Ford" trademark at the neutral point. Be sure this mark is at the top. Many pilots accustomed to "stick" control forget this detail entirely, and take off with the ailerons off center.

The fundamentals of safe flying are the same regardless of the size of the airplane, or the number of engines with which it is propelled. Speed means safety—all pilots know this—yet in some cases there is a tendency to rely too much on the wide margin of power which is provided in modern airplanes, and to forget the simple rules of safe flying which are just as true today as they were in the early days of flight. Pilots should never overlook the safety factor of starting from the extreme end of the runway when taking off.

Two Engine Performance

The Ford tri-motor monoplane flying on any two engines will climb very satisfactorily and fly level continuously at the full gross load which is named in its Department of Commerce license. It is provided with directional controls which allow it to be flown straight, or to turn it in any direction with one outboard engine stopped. In any field of reasonable size it can be taken off with its full specified gross load on the two outboard engines alone, although this is not recommended in transport operations. Yet even with these advantages, which allow the airplane to be flown over any terrain without thought of mechanical failure or forced landings, there is still the necessity for careful handling and sound, conservative judgment on the part of the pilot.

When considering the operation of a three engine airplane on two engines, it should be remembered that it is very simple to fly along at cruising speed, cut one of the engines, and fly level or climb on the two remaining engines. It is quite a different matter to have an engine fail unexpectedly in a steep take-off, where the ship is at its maximum angle of climb, especially if the ship is in a turn and it is the engine on the inside of the turn that fails.

Every airplane has its maximum performance, no matter whether it has one engine or a dozen. If a tri-motor airplane is held at its maximum rate of climb (*) on three engines, and one engine stops, then it *cannot* continue along its former flight path, even though it can climb perfectly well—at a lower rate of course—and at the angle of climb and air speed which give it its best two engine performance. In some cases the angle of climb which gives the airplane its maximum climbing performance on *three* engines puts the ship into an attitude where, should an outboard engine fail, it would be difficult to maintain a safe margin of flying speed and

(*) Maximum angle and maximum rate of climb should not be confused.

adequate directional control without some loss in altitude. It is especially important to remember this in taking off.

The fundamentals of safe flying are the same regardless of the size and classification of an airplane. With any airplane—climbing steeply near the ground at maximum engine performance, does not afford a wide margin of safety in the event of engine failure.

All pilots of multi-engined airplanes should thoroughly familiarize themselves with the flying characteristics of the airplane on the various two engine combinations. To do this requires practice of two engine flying, with close attention to the airspeed indicator, rate of climb indicator, and altimeter. No figures on the best climbing speed can be given here as they vary widely with the model of the airplane, the load carried, and the altitude at which the plane is flown.

Directional Control

Pilots should be thoroughly familiar with the directional control characteristics of three engine airplanes. When flying on the center engine and only one outboard engine, there is naturally considerable eccentricity of thrust tending to turn the airplane in the direction of the engine which is stopped. This force can be overcome with the rudder—in fact, the Ford tri-motor, as previously stated can, within the ordinary range of airspeeds, be easily turned to the left with the right engine stopped, and vice versa. However, it must be remembered that the effectiveness of any control surface depends upon the speed of the airplane. There is a minimum air speed below which the rudder rapidly loses its effectiveness when holding a ship straight with two engines and one outboard engine stopped. Pilots should learn the possibilities and limitations of the directional controls under these conditions.

When flying on all three engines, it is possible, through reckless or incompetent handling, to put the ship into a position—such as a steep climbing turn near the ground—where, should the lower engine fail, there would be great difficulty not only in maintaining the altitude already gained, but in preventing a turn toward the engine which has stopped. The solution to this problem does not lie with the builder of the plane. Any airplane, no matter how excellent its performance, has its very definite limitations and can be abused. It is the pilot's duty and responsibility to know his ship thoroughly, and to avoid situations where engine failure would constitute a hazard.

Do Not Use Brakes Unnecessarily

Brakes are provided to facilitate taxiing and to stop the ship in an emergency. To avoid premature tire wear the brakes should not be used unnecessarily. When operating an airplane with no load in the cabin, the brakes must be used very cautiously. To avoid undue twisting on the landing wheel, never lock the brake on one wheel and use it as a pivot. Always let the wheel to which the brake is applied, roll slightly (particularly on soft ground).

Engine Instruction Book Should be Carefully Studied

The engine instruction book furnished with each airplane describes in detail the correct instrument readings; fuel and oil specifications and requirements, starting, cold weather operation, and periodic inspection. It also covers the disassembly, overhaul, and assembly of the engines. To deviate from the recommendations contained in the engine instruction book is to invite serious trouble. Every pilot should make a careful study of the engine handbook.

Use Oil and Gasoline of Correct Specifications

It is particularly important that only fuel and oil of the correct specifications be used. In an emergency, when it becomes absolutely necessary to use gasoline of automobile grade, the engines should be throttled down as low as possible while cruising. Anti-detonating compounds should be used only with the approval of the engine manufacturer. It should be unnecessary to remind pilots that all gasoline, from any source whatever, should be strained through chamois or felt before it is put into the tank.

Gasoline and Oil Lines

To avoid accumulation of dirt and water from condensation, the gasoline lines, oil lines and strainers should be frequently cleaned.

Carburetor Operating Temperatures

The function of the carburetor air preheater and hot spots above the carburetor is to supply sufficient heat to more properly volatilize the fuel. When a liquid such as gasoline passes from liquid to gaseous form, it is necessary to supply a considerable amount of heat; this is called the latent heat of vaporization. The proper place to supply this heat would be at the carburetor nozzle, but as this is impractical, the heat is supplied either by preheating or directly above the carburetor in the hot spot. The drop in temperature of the air through the carburetor, due to the absorption of heat to vaporize the fuel, may be as much as 50° F. If insufficient heat is supplied, the fuel in vaporizing takes the heat from the incoming air. Cold air cannot hold as much water vapor in suspension as warm air; as a result the water vapor is deposited on the walls of the manifold and carburetor mixing chamber. If the air is cooled below 32° F., the water freezes, choking up the induction system at this point and freezing the throttles.

This action may occur in the temperate zone during the early fall months even at low altitudes, or in the tropics at high altitudes, depending largely on the humidity. Cold air intakes should be used only during warm weather and at low altitudes.

Operators are cautioned to study their air conditions carefully, as this physical phenomenon has in several instances been mistaken for a faulty mechanical carburetor control.

"V" Type Windshield

In cases of tropical storms, where heavy downpours of rain occur for short periods, it may become necessary to open the rear sliding glass of the windshield. In such cases, it is recommended that the pilot wear amber colored goggles, straight lens type.

GENERAL DESCRIPTION OF THE
FORD   ALL-METAL   MONOPLANE

THE Ford tri-motor is an all-metal cantilever high wing cabin mono-plane. It is constructed from heat treated aluminum alloy channels riveted together with aluminum alloy rivets and covered with a corrugated aluminum coated alloy sheet. Aluminum alloy is an exceptionally strong light weight metal. It has the strength of steel yet only about one-third the weight.

Fuselage

The fuselage is basically rectangular in shape with a rounded deck. It is constructed entirely of aluminum alloy with Alclad covering. The structure is formed into economical sections from aluminum alloy sheets. The sections are assembled by means of gussets and aluminum alloy rivets. Alclad sheet consists of a heat-treated strong aluminum alloy base protected from corrosion by smooth, dense surface layers of high purity aluminum, alloyed with the core.

Cabin Interior and Equipment

The interior of the cabin in the standard planes is covered with Ford Aero board wall covering. Aero board is made up of two thin sheets of aluminum with a balsa wood core. This provides an excellent surface for the interior decorations and in addition adds to the sound-proofing and cleanliness of the cabin. The sub-floor is made from $\frac{1}{4}''$ veneer—it is mounted on the channel frame work. A durable covering is cemented to the top of the floor.

Passenger chairs are furnished in both wicker and aluminum and are covered with leather in color to match the interior of the cabin. Windows are of non-shatterable glass equipped with individual shades. Electric lights are placed above the windows for the convenience of passengers. The toilet compartment is located at the rear of the cabin. Entrance is obtained through a door in the rear cabin wall. Space for luggage is provided in the wing compartments on both sides of the fuselage. Doors in the cabin ceiling provide access to the wing compartments. Special cabin equipment includes berths, arm chairs, radio, typewriter desk, ice boxes, cupboards, and carpets.

Adequate cabin ventilation is secured by means of special ventilators and by opening the side windows. In cold weather heated air is provided through registers in the floor.

Pilot's Compartment

The pilot's control compartment is located in the front section of the plane. It is separated from the passenger cabin by a door. The control compartment is equipped with dual wheel controls together with a complete set of instruments.

Wing

The wing is an internally braced structure of monoplane design. It is composed of three units: the root or center section above the fuselage, and the two wing tips. The root section is a high lift airfoil section of constant thickness. The wing tips are tapered in both plan and front elevation, changing gradually from the root section to a high speed thin section at the extreme tips.

The wing structure consists of three main spars. To distribute the loads among the spars, the spars are interconnected at regular intervals by means of rib trussing. There are 22 rib trusses on each side of the fuselage. Five auxiliary spars located transversely and intermediately between the main spars carry the loads to the rib trusses and thence to the main spars. The entire wing is covered with corrugated alclad, riveted to the spars. All rivets in the wing can be easily inspected, no "blind" rivets are used. All spars and rib truss sections are formed from aluminum alloy sheet. The sections are riveted together by means of gusset plates into a rigid structure of homogeneous material proportionately designed to permit uniform deflection.

The gasoline tanks are placed in the wings between spars Nos. 1 and 2, the fuel load being carried on these spars.

Ailerons

The ailerons are of the airfoil counterbalanced type. Their controls are of the cable and horn design, the cables being carried inside of the wings along the front spar to the fuselage and thence to the control wheels.

Control Surfaces

The general size and shape of the tail surfaces afford excellent control throughout the entire range of action. The stabilizer is rectangular in shape, built upon two main spars which are connected with diagonal trussing. This structure is covered with corrugated alclad which is riveted to the spars and rib trussing. The stabilizer is easily adjusted in flight by means of a control placed above and behind the pilot's seat in the cockpit. The elevators are carried on the stabilizer through hinge bearings equipped with self-aligning ball bearings. The controls for the rudder and elevators are of the cable and horn type. The cables run through fair leads on the outside of the fuselage. This arrangement permits maximum inspection.

The surface controls are arranged in the conventional position just forward of the pilot and mechanic's seats. They are operated through a column having dual wheel controls. The aileron cable leads are continuous throughout the columns. Numerous inspection windows are provided near the points where the cables travel over the pulleys. The bearings are equipped with pressure lubricators.

Landing Gear

The landing gear is of the wide tread split axle type. It consists of a specially designed axle with rear brace tube and shock absorber strut. Disc type rubber shock absorbers are used in the compression members, giving a total compression of 9 inches to this member. The fittings on the ends of the axle tubes are secured by the flash weld method developed by the Ford Motor Company. Maximum tube strength is obtained in the weld by this process. The axle tubes are cadmium coated and boiled in oil for twenty minutes. When the boiling operation is completed, the tubes are drained and the holes plugged.

Brakes

The brakes are hydraulically operated. They are of ample capacity and unusually efficient. The linings operate in a "V" type brake drum on the wheel rim. The braking torque is carried from the wheel rim directly to the brake reaction plate. This construction prevents any stressing of the wheel spokes. The brake control lever is mounted between the pilot's seats; it operates upon the cylinders for each wheel. The master cylinders are located beneath the floor in the pilot's compartment. Copper, double annealed tubing, connects these cylinders with the two brake actuating cylinders which are located on the brake reaction plate. Each brake actuating cylinder controls two linked shoes which contact with the wheel drum. The control lever in the cockpit is so located with respect to the cylinders beneath the floor that on pulling the lever directly aft the brakes are equally applied to both wheels. On pulling diagonally aft and to the right, the right wheel only is affected and similarly by pulling diagonally aft and to the left the left wheel only is affected. This method assures perfect ground control.

With normal load distribution in the cabin, the Ford plane can be landed with full braking effort, providing the landing field surface is conducive to proper braking action. On soft landing surfaces, care must be used when applying the brakes to prevent nosing down.

Tires

The landing wheel tires are 40 x 10 cord type; the tail wheel tire is 20 x 4. The recommended inflation pressure of the former is 60 pounds, the latter 50 pounds.

Tail Wheel

The tail wheel is sprung on rubber shock absorbers in the same manner as the landing gear. It is built on the principle of a trailing wheel with rubber core snubbers secured on each side. These snubbers keep the wheel in a fore and aft position except when sufficient pressure is exercised to move it sideways. The tail wheel has 165 degree radius of action. It is prevented from going further by rubber bumpers attached to each side of the fuselage. A steering fork is provided to hook over the tail wheel axle so that the plane can be easily moved about in field or hangar. The fork is carried in the aft end of the fuselage and is furnished as standard equipment.

Instrument Equipment

All instruments, both navigation and engine, are of standard makes. A complete list and description of the instruments is contained on page 86. The instrument panel is electrically lighted, the amount of light being controlled by a rheostat. A drain is provided in the air speed tubes, located just behind the pilot's seat, for draining any water or condensation that might form in the lines.

Power Plant

The power plant consists of three engines, namely, the center engine mounted at the front of the fuselage, and the two outboard engines attached to the underside of the wing. Each engine is enclosed in a separate nacelle. The nacelles also contain the oil tanks, oil lines, starter, carburetors, controls, etc.

The engine mounts are made of Chrome Molybdenum tubing. This method of trussing provides minimum weight. The intersection of the tubes in the mount are reinforced by gusset plates.

The entire mount is boiled in oil inside and out, the oil entering the interior of the tubes through small holes at the end of each tube. After draining, the holes are plugged with self-threading screws. To prevent the steel tube members rusting or corroding, the exterior of the mount is given a coat of aluminum paint.

The cowling is made of half hard aluminum and is carried on a steel tube framework, supported by lugs on the engine mount.

The propellers are of the all metal type. The blades are machined from aluminum alloy forgings and assembled in a forged steel hub.

The oil tubes are made of aluminum. To remove all internal stresses and prevent crystallization, the tubes are annealed after bending.

An oil strainer is provided in the top of the tanks in planes equipped with J-6 engines. (Planes equipped with Wasp and Hornet engines have a large strainer in the crankcase.) In the center of the strainer is a tapped hole of sufficient size to accommodate the oil temperature bulb. The strainer in the tanks must be removed and cleaned after every ten hours' flight.

All oil tanks on commercial planes are provided with an expansion space at the top of the tank from which a vent line is carried to the atmosphere. On military ships, the vent is connected to the crankcase. The oil flow through the tank is so arranged that oil enters the tank at one end and flows the full length of the tank before passing out at the sump. This arrangement materially assists in cooling. To assist in cooling the oil, tanks for J-6 engines are provided with cooling tubes in the bottom of the tanks.

All oil tanks are of welded sheet aluminum equipped with baffles to insure maximum strength and to control the oil flow through the tanks. Standard air service rubber hose and fittings together with durable hose clamps are used throughout the oil system.

The starter and primer control is located on the outer side of each outboard cowling.

Hand inertia starters are furnished as standard equipment. Electric (or other type) starters and generators are furnished as special equipment when desired.

Instruments are provided for each outboard engine for indicating oil temperature, oil pressure, and engine R. P. M. The instruments are mounted on a strut above the engine nacelle, facing the pilot and are illuminated electrically.

As special equipment, fire extinguishers can be installed with a separate control to each engine.

Fuel System

With the exception of planes equipped with a Wasp center engine, the gravity feed type fuel system is used. Planes equipped with a Wasp center engine are provided with a fuel pump. This is necessary to insure sufficient flow into the high head carburetor used with the Wasp engine.

The three aluminum welded fuel tanks (one large main tank at both sides of the fuselage and a smaller emergency tank located over the fuselage) are placed in the center section of the wing. They are filled through rubber-capped holes located in the upper wing surface, access to which is obtained through a trap door located in the cabin ceiling. The filler is fitted internally with a removable screen and externally with a splash trough. The trough drains outside of the wing. The tank outlet stand pipe is built into the sump so as to trap a considerable amount of water. The trapped water can be expelled through a drain cock placed in the sump. This cock is also used to empty the tank.

The annealed copper fuel lines are supported by clips on the airplane structure. Hose connections, with brass inner-liners, are placed wherever differences in vibration periods of the several parts of the supporting structure necessitate a flexible joint in the line.

Two three-way valves and one two-way valve control the fuel flow from any tank to either of the outboard engines. Dials and levers for the valves (all of which have remote controls) are located directly over the pilot's head on the rear wall of the cockpit. The valve controlling the center engine fuel line (either gravity or pump) is located on the wall of the pilot's compartment to the left of the pilot's seat.

A standard strainer is placed at the lowest point in each of the lines to the three engines.

The priming system consists of a pump, a valve and $\frac{1}{8}$-inch annealed tubing. The tubing leads to the engine. The pump for the center engine is located on the instrument panel. The outboard pump is located in the outboard engine nacelle.

SPECIFICATIONS

General Dimensions

	4-AT-E	5-AT-C
Span—Overall	74 ft. 0 in.	77 ft. 10 in.
Length—Overall	49 ft. 10 in.	49 ft. 10 in.
Wing Area	785 sq. ft.	835 sq. ft.
Height	12 ft. 8 in.	13 ft. 8 in.
Wheel Tread	16 ft. 9 in.	18 ft. 7 in.

Performance

	4-AT-E	5-AT-C
High Speed	130 M. P. H.	135 M. P. H.
Cruising Speed	110 M. P. H.	115 M. P. H.
Stalling Speed	58 M. P. H.	64 M. P. H.
Range—Normal	560 Miles	510 Miles
—Maximum	670 Miles	650 Miles
Service Ceiling	14,500 ft.	17,000 ft.
Absolute Ceiling	16,000 ft.	18,500 ft.
Gliding Ratio	9.7 to 1	8.7 to 1
Rate of climb at sea level	950 F. P. M.	950 F. P. M.

Weights—Loads—Tank Capacities, Etc.

(Completely equipped for passenger service, with standard equipment)

	4-AT-E	5-AT-C
Weight Empty	6,500 lbs.	7,500 lbs.
Useful Load	3,630 lbs.	6,000 lbs.
Total Weight Loaded	10,130 lbs.	13,500 lbs.
Gasoline Capacity—Normal	231 gal.	277 gal.
—Maximum	281 gal.	355 gal.
Oil Capacity	30 gal.	34 gal.
Wing Loading—lbs. per sq. ft.	12.90	16.10
Power Loading—lbs. per H. P.—		
1 Engine	....	31.8
2 Engines	16.88	15.9
3 Engines	11.25	10.60

Cabin Data

	4-AT-E	5-AT-C
Capacity—Width, Average	4 ft. 6 in.	4 ft. 6 in.
—Height, Average	6 ft. 0 in.	6 ft. 0 in.
—Length, Average	16 ft. 3 in.	18 ft. 9 in.
—Volume	420 cu. ft.	529 cu. ft.
Cabin Floor Area	87.2 sq. ft.	100 sq. ft.
Wash Room—Volume	68 cu. ft.	
Passenger Seats, removable	11	13
Baggage Space	33 cu. ft.	38.5 cu. ft.

Cabin lined with Ford Aero Board — Choice of color combinations. Cabin illumination—Side lights—Dome lights. Passenger chairs— Reed or aluminum—Upholstered to match interior. Window Shades— Color to match interior trim. Non-shatterable Window Glass. Cabin Heater.

Power

Engines......................	3, Wright J-6	3, P. & W. Wasp
Total Power..................	900 H. P.	1,275 H. P.
Propellers...................	Metal	Metal
Starters.....................	Hand Inertia	Hand Inertia

EQUIPMENT

Standard Equipment—All Models

Airplane exterior trim—customer's choice of standard colors. Pilot's Compartment (Color)

Brakes

Hydraulic

Storage Battery

13 Plate (Aircraft)

Instruments

1—Altimeter
1—Magnetic Compass
1—Turn and Bank Indicator
1—Air Speed Indicator
1—Rate of Climb Indicator
3—Oil Pressure Gauges
3—Oil Temperature Gauges
3—Tachometers
1—Clock
3—Engine Primers
4—Instrument Lights
1—Fuel Pressure Gauge
2—Gasoline Gauges
1—Stabilizer Indicator

Toilet Compartment and Equipment

1—Toilet
1—Towel Rack
1—Waste Towel Rack
1—Wash Bowl
1— Water Tank
1--First Aid Kit
1—Soap Dispenser

Miscellaneous

Floor Covering
Hat Rack
Two Fire Extinguishers
Tail Wheel
One Tail Wheel Maneuvering Fork
One Booster Magneto
Two Pilots' Safety Belts
Three Navigation Lights
Three Engine Covers
Fuel Funnel
Three Mooring Ropes
Three Mooring Stakes
Starting Crank
Two Tool Kits
One Wheel Cover Wrench
One Wheel Fender Nut Wrench
One Tool Box
Engine and Plane Instruction Books
Engine Log Books
Plane Log Book

Special Equipment—(Installed only on request)

The following additional equipment may be obtained at a reasonable cost, increasing the empty weight of the plane by the amount shown:

	4-AT-E	5-AT-C
Auxiliary engine carburetor air heaters with controls to cockpit, taking pre-heated air from a jacket about the exhaust pipe	Not Used	50 lbs.
Super Cabin Heater, designed for winter use in temperate and colder climates	50 lbs.	60 lbs.
Additional Bevel Gear Drive for external electric gun motor starters	Not Used	35 lbs.
Electric Inertia Starters—This includes the difference in weight between these starters and the hand inertia starters. The weight of the cable, controls, and extra battery weight	100 lbs.	100 lbs.
For maximum fuel capacity, additional weight of tank, straps, and gauge	50 lbs.	75 lbs.
Landing lights built into wing, with mounts and cable, also extra weight for heavy duty battery	55 lbs.	55 lbs.
Two parachute flare holders with control in pilot's cockpit	20 lbs.	20 lbs.

Earth Inductor Compass.............	35 lbs.	35 lbs.
Primers installed in cockpit...........	8 lbs.	8 lbs.
Thermos Carafe—1 quart, for drinking water.........................	8 lbs.	8 lbs.
Drinking cup container..............	1 lb.	1 lb.
Cabin Altimeter and Air Speed Indicator with piping....................	5 lbs.	5 lbs.
One Generator, with wiring...........	31 lbs.	31 lbs.
Radio Shielding, Ignition System only..	12 lbs.	12 lbs.
Three-passenger folding bench in place of one chair near door adds..........	28 lbs.	28 lbs.
Extension on engine covers for heating adds...........................	2 lbs.	2 lbs.
Locker—Provision for Steward Supplies..	20 lbs.	20 lbs.

The Ford Motor Company reserves the right to make changes in design or to make additions or improvements upon its product without imposing any obligation upon itself to install the same on its product previously manufactured.

Part II

SHIPMENT of AIRCRAFT

Erection Procedure
Instructions for Starting

SHIPMENT OF AIRCRAFT
PLANE IS DIVIDED INTO UNITS — EACH UNIT
SEPARATELY PACKED

WHEN shipped by freight or boat the various major assemblies of the plane are divided into units. Each unit is then separately packed into a sealed packing box.

The shipment of the complete monoplane consists of the following units:

1.   Fuselage unit—For shipping purposes this unit includes the cockpit controls, center engine mount, cowling, oil tank, exhaust manifold, cabin heater and controls, instruments, and the complete cabin. The dimensions of the box used in crating this unit are approximately 6' 7" x 10' x 44' for all model planes.

2.   The center engine unit includes the carburetor and all equipment. This box is approximately 46¾" x 52¼" x 54 for the Wright engine and approximately 56" x 56" x 50" for the Wasp engine.

3.   The wing center section unit includes fuel tanks, baggage compartments, engine controls and gasoline lines installed. This box is approximately 3' 6" x 17' 6" x 14' 6" for 4AT models and approximately 3' 6" x 21' x 14' 6" for other models.

4.   The wing tip section unit includes the aileron, and navigation lamp installed. The boxes for shipping this section are approximately 3' 6" x 30' 6" x 14' 8".

5.   The outboard engine units include the complete assembly of the engine mount with engine, oil tank, instruments, exhaust manifold, cowling, and mount side braces. The shipping box is approximately 11' x 10' x 6' 6" for all models.

6.   The landing gear unit includes axle tube, wheels and tires, rear compression struts, shock absorbers, brake tension struts, and fenders. These parts are placed in the fuselage box.

7.   The tail unit includes the elevators, vertical fin, rudder, horizontal stabilizer, with brace tubes and guide wires. These parts together with the tail wheel unit, shock absorber, wheel and tire are also included in the fuselage box.

All universal links and bolts are attached to their respective members. When assembling the units, the bolts furnished must be used. Many of these bolts are specially made from heat treated alloy steel and must not be replaced with commercial bolts, as commercial bolts do not have the required strength and close tolerances. A complete list of these bolts is given on page 110.

Instructions for proper removal of units from boxes are noted on the outside of each box.

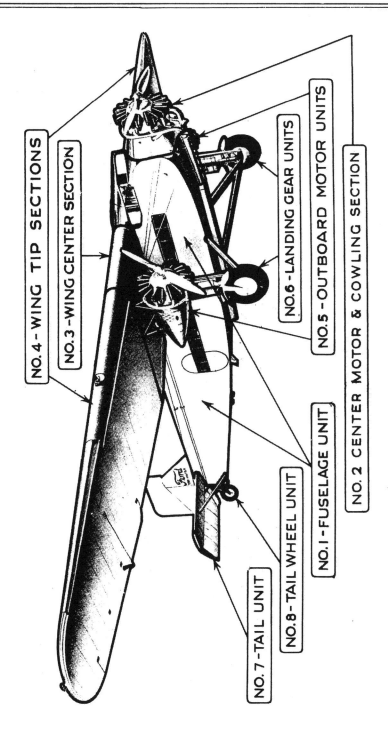

NO.4 – WING TIP SECTIONS

NO.3 – WING CENTER SECTION

NO.6 – LANDING GEAR UNITS

NO.5 – OUTBOARD MOTOR UNITS

NO.2 CENTER MOTOR & COWLING SECTION

NO.1 – FUSELAGE UNIT

NO.8 – TAIL WHEEL UNIT

NO.7 – TAIL UNIT

Figure 4—For Shipping and Assembly Purposes the Plane is Divided into Units

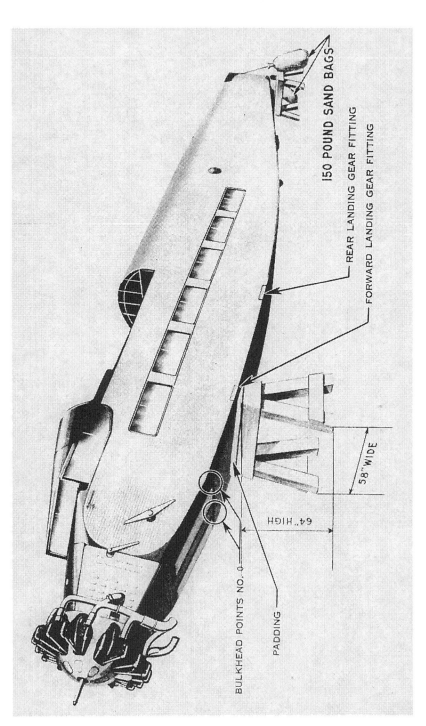

Figure 5—Assembly Position of the Fuselage

ERECTION PROCEDURE

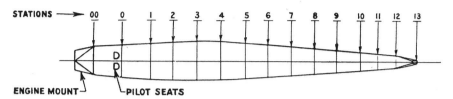

Figure 6
Stations or bulkheads used in the Ford monoplane

Figure 6 gives the numbers of the various stations used in the construction of the Ford monoplane. These stations are frequently referred to as bulkheads.

The first step in the erection of the airplane is the proper placing of the fuselage to facilitate the mounting of the various units. Briefly, erection consists of mounting the wing center section on the fuselage; hanging the outboard engine units; attaching landing gear; mounting wing tip sections; assembly of empanage, tail wheel unit, and final rigging of all controls.

The fuselage as shipped weighs approximately 2000 pounds. When handling with a crane, the fuselage should be supported on a well padded

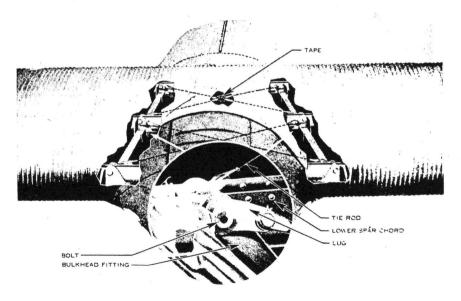

Figure 7

"I" beam, placed just aft of No. 0 bulkhead, so that wooden blocks placed inside of the fuselage will rest over the steel beam. No special precautions are necessary when handled by a group of men, there being sufficient local strength due to the all-metal construction, so that the hands may be placed anywhere. The fuselage should be placed on a horse with the tail low and anchored with ropes and stakes, or sand bags as shown in Fig. 5. Anchoring the fuselage in this manner prevents it from nosing over.

The horse should be approximately 58 inches wide and 64 inches high. It should have a wide base and have sufficient strength to support 6,000 pounds safely. The cross bar should be well padded. The horse must be placed directly under the forward landing gear fittings so that its cross bar coincides with the cross member of the bulkhead as revealed by the rivets at that point. (See Fig. 5).

After the fuselage has been securely placed in position the center section of the wing is mounted. If the center section is handled with a crane, the cables should be attached at the outer end fittings. If no crane is available the center section can be lifted on the fuselage by a group of men. The attachment is made through six female fittings at the upper end of the fuselage bulkhead verticals (see Fig. 7). Before the bolts are passed through the bulkhead fitting and the lower chord members of the wing spar, the diagonal tie rods of the drag structure must be installed. The tie rods are fitted with lugs which serve as washers under the head of the bolts and nut. The spacers on the wing bolts must be placed inside of the wing chord so that when the bolt is tightened the chord channels will not be crushed. Next adjust the tie rods for uniform tension, tightening each rod until it is just snug. To reduce wear in service the tie rods must be taped at points of contact. (See Fig. 8).

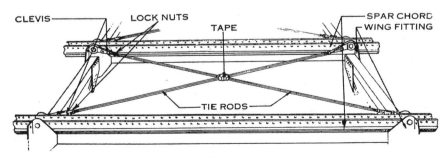

Figure 8

INSTALLING OUTBOARD ENGINE ASSEMBLIES

The right and left hand assemblies are recognized by the engine braces that are placed on the inboard or fuselage side. The units are attached by first bolting them to the wing at the outer edge. If chain falls are not available, a tripod of heavy timbers, approximately 12 feet high, with a block and tackle, can be used to support the engines. A cable is passed through the lifting eyes located on each side to the rear of top center cylinder. Care must be taken not to damage leading edge of wing. (To prevent the plane tipping over when mounting an outboard engine, extreme care must be taken to securely anchor the opposite side of the plane). The front and rear diagonal braces are next bolted in place (although these engine braces have adjustable ends, no adjustment is necessary, the required adjustment having been made during the final assembly at the factory). The fuel lines, engine controls and ignition wires can now be connected. (See Fig. 9). When connecting engine controls the special clevis pins furnished must be used. These special pins prevent excessive movement in the engine control rods.

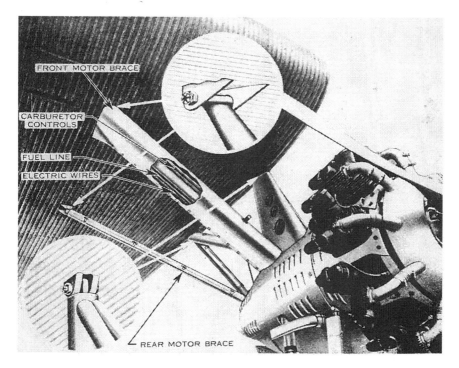

Figure 9

ATTACHING LANDING GEAR

After the engine mounts have been bolted to the wing the shock absorber strut is attached to the lower end of the engine mount vertical through a universal link located on the strut.

The axle tubes with the wheel and brake assemblies are then assembled to the fuselage and shock absorber strut. The diagonal lug on the collar near the wheel should face the rear. A universal link connects the axle tube with the forward fuselage fitting.

The rear brace can now be placed by bolting it to the diagonal lug of the axle collar and to the rear fuselage universal link. The three jaw fittings are

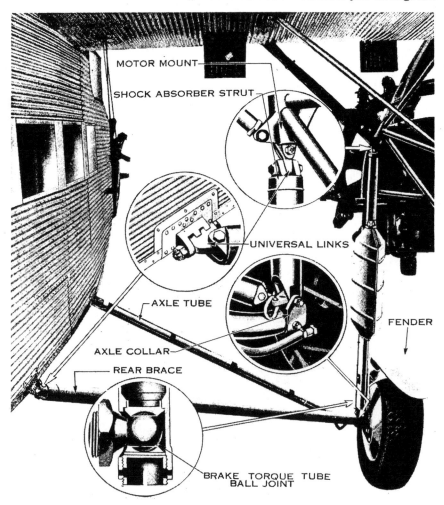

MOTOR MOUNT

SHOCK ABSORBER STRUT

UNIVERSAL LINKS

AXLE TUBE

FENDER

AXLE COLLAR

REAR BRACE

BRAKE TORQUE TUBE
BALL JOINT

Figure 10

designed to permit variation of toe-in of wheels. (See page 45 for description of toe-in.) The correct position of the jaw is shown in Fig. 10. Install fittings in exact relative position as shown. When installing these parts, all joints on the landing gear members should be well lubricated with a heavy oil or grease.

The hydraulic brake assembly is next connected (complete details of the hydraulic brake system are described on page 48). The fender assemblies are next mounted on the landing gear. The cap on the outside axle end is removed and the fender assembly fitted to the axle. The cap is then replaced, locked with a set screw, and safety wired. The inner ends of the brackets are next bolted to the shock absorber strut.

NOTE: The terms "right" and "left" refer to the view point of an observer sitting in the airplane facing the direction of flight.

At its lower end the brake strut is fitted to the ball stud which extends from the front of the brake beam. Adjustment is made by means of the end plug in the strut. The fit should be snug yet sufficiently free to prevent binding. The joint should be well packed with grease. The upper end of the strut is then bolted through a universal link to the engine mount ring.

The assembly of the landing gear is now complete and the plane may be removed from the horse by lowering it with jacks placed under the axle collars.

ATTACHING WING TIP SECTIONS

The wing tip sections with the ailerons mounted can now be raised into position and bolted to the wing center section. (See Fig. 11). When bolting these parts together, let the outer end of the wing tip point downward, then insert the lower bolts first in spars No. 2 and No. 3. This provides a hinging action which allows the top fittings to slip easily into place. When the wing tips have been bolted to the center section and the air speed and other connections have been made, cover the gap between the wing tips and center section with the metal strap, provided for this purpose. The strap is tightened by means of turnbuckles.

Figure 11

MOUNTING TAIL SURFACES

The stabilizer with the elevators attached, slides into the fuselage decking. It is connected to the front of the decking by means of two hinges. (Do not draw hinge bolts down tightly as it will cause the hinges to bind.) The rear end is connected to the stabilizer adjustment screw through a link. (See Fig. 12). The stabilizer brace tubes are bolted to the fitting on the fuselage side. The ball socket at the stabilizer end is securely clamped and then lubricated. No adjustment of this strut is required. The fin and

Figure 12

rudder assembly are next mounted by bolting the fin to the fuselage deck. The fin post is bolted to the tail post of the fuselage. The fin brace wire is connected to the stabilizer beam by a turnbuckle. The fin is rigged perpendicular to the stabilizer.

CONNECTING SURFACE CONTROLS

The aileron control cables are connected to the ailerons and coiled at the intersection of the tip section with the wing center section. It is possible for a small man to crawl through the center section, reach this coil and place the cable in the fair leads. Connection of the cables through turnbuckles is made at the fuselage.

The elevator and rudder control cables are attached to their horns on the outside of the cockpit. These cables are passed over their proper pulleys on the center spar of the wing center section, through the upper wing surface and fuselage fair leads, to the rudder and elevator horns. (See Fig. 13).

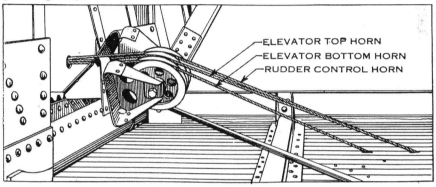

ELEVATOR TOP HORN
ELEVATOR BOTTOM HORN
RUDDER CONTROL HORN

Figure 13

MOUNTING TAIL WHEEL

The tail wheel is attached to the rear of the fuselage. (See Fig. 14). The universal links are held in place with two bolts provided with pressure lubricator fittings. The bottom bolt is mounted with the fitting toward the top and the top bolt with the fitting toward the bottom. All joints must be well lubricated and free. The shock cord is attached to the bottom fitting of the stabilizer brace tube on the fuselage. This cord should have even tension, so that the tail wheel will track.

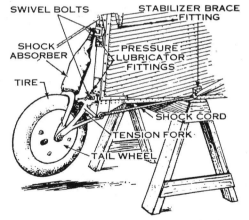

SWIVEL BOLTS
STABILIZER BRACE FITTING
SHOCK ABSORBER
PRESSURE LUBRICATOR FITTINGS
TIRE
SHOCK CORD
TENSION FORK
TAIL WHEEL

Figure 14

INSTRUCTIONS FOR STARTING

WITH the ignition switch off the following points should be carefully checked before starting the engines:

1. Check over all nuts and bolts on each engine and mount; see that they are tight and properly locked.

2. Check the propeller hub nuts—be sure they have been drawn down tightly and cottered.

3. Lubricate the valve gear on the engines.

4. See that ground wires are connected at the magnetos.

5. Remove spark plugs or dummy plugs and turn engine over ten or twelve times to expel any oil.

6. Replace spark plugs. If the spark plugs were installed when the engine was received, wash them in gasoline before replacing.

7. Fill the oil tank with a sufficient quantity of oil for the run (minimum amount 2 gallons), and see that all lines are clear.

8. Fill the gasoline tanks with the proper grade of gasoline. See that gasoline is supplied to the carburetor and that all lines are tight. See that the carburetors do not drip gasoline.

9. Operate the throttle and mixture controls and inspect the levers on the carburetor to make certain that they touch the stop at both ends of the travel without restriction.

10. See that the tachometer and pressure gauge are properly connected and that oil temperature thermometer bulb is in place.

11. **Turn the engine over by hand to see that everything is clear.**

12. See that priming lines and pumps are properly connected and in working order.

STARTING

Having completed the pre-starting inspection the engine is ready to start and should be handled as follows:

1. Give the engine several strokes of the priming pump. Experience is necessary to determine the proper amount of prime for each type of motor. About five or six strokes of the pump is usually required.

   Do not make a practice of priming the engine more than necessary. Excessive priming has a tendency to wash the oil off the cylinder walls and cause scoring or seizing of the sleeves and pistons. In cold weather the engine requires more priming than in warm weather. A hot engine does not ordinarily require priming. BE SURE PRIMER SHUT-OFF VALVE IS CLOSED AFTER PRIMING, OTHERWISE THE ENGINE MAY BE DAMAGED.

2. Set the throttle to approximately $\frac{1}{8}$ open and the mixture to full rich. The booster magneto plug on the right hand side of control knee must be plugged in to panel for corresponding engine. Master ignition switch must be in "on" position when starting.

3. Operate the starter and allow the engine to turn over a full revolution. Then turn the ignition switch to the start position and operate the booster magneto. The engines used in the planes have a fixed spark setting and, due to the fact that the spark is always in the advanced position, it is very important when starting that the engine be turned over rapidly. This lessens any possibility of a "kick back."

   For the same reason do not permit the starter gear to remain engaged at low starter speeds.

4. If the engine fails to start after several attempts, prime again and repeat. If the engine is overprimed turn off the ignition switch, open the throttle wide and turn the engine backward several revolutions by hand. When doing this be certain that the ignition switch is off.

5. In extremely cold weather the oil should be heated before filling the oil tank. If the engine fails to start after a reasonable number of attempts, consult chapter on troubles in engine instruction book to ascertain possible cause. For further information on the engine refer to the engine instruction book.

Running in New Engines

The first 10 hours in service are the most important in the engine's life. Great care must be taken to break the engine in properly. The section on operation in the engine handbook should be read carefully. In the following paragraphs, a detailed plan of running in the engine is described. This procedure should be followed to insure long life.

After starting, run slowly (not over 750 R. P. M.) for five minutes. Then run at approximately 1000 R. P. M. until the oil outlet temperature reaches 40° C. (104° F.) or 30° C. (86° F.) in extremely cold weather (a cold engine does not always fire properly; adjust throttle to a speed which results in smooth running). Increase speed to 1200 R. P. M. and run for five minutes. Increase speed to 1400 R. P. M. and run for ten minutes. Increase the speed to 1500 R. P. M. and run for fifteen minutes. Slowly open to full throttle and leave in this position only long enough to see that the engine is running smoothly and firing properly, checking magnetos and mixture control. Reduce the speed by slowly closing the throttle. Use at least three minutes in getting throttle back to idling position. Check idling for running at 300 to 350 R. P. M. by adjusting throttle stop, if necessary. Adjust the idling mixture, getting this as rich as possible and still have a smooth running engine which does not "lope." This provides for a cold engine idling properly. Check oil and fuel pressure at idling.

It is desirable to run the engine on the ground at 1450 R. P. M. for one hour before the ship is flown. This serves to give the engine a final run-in and is a precautionary check of the installation. The one hour run-in is the minimum advisable and when possible, a longer time should be allowed.

After this run-in, the oil strainer should be cleaned to remove any dirt that may have gotten into the fuel tanks or pipes.

Part III

SERVICE INSTRUCTIONS

Fuselage
Wings
Tail Surfaces
Wheels
Brakes
Surface Controls

SERVICE INSTRUCTIONS

THE FUSELAGE

General

EXCEPT where abnormal usage has damaged the metal, no servicing of the fuselage is necessary.

When walking inside rear of fuselage, care must be taken to step on the walkway provided for this purpose.

Do not walk on top of the fuselage.

A box provided for tools, etc., is located at the rear of the wash room—do not overload this box or place other articles in this section.

Cabin

The interior finish of the cabin on the passenger airplanes consists of a decorative covered sound and heat insulating board. In case removal is necessary to gain access to the structure or wiring, the board can be removed in sections as revealed by the trim strips. The cabin interior may be washed with a mild soap and luke warm water and polished with any good grade automobile or wax polish. Do not use a hose to wash interior. The chairs are fastened to the floor by means of sockets at each chair leg; these sockets must be kept securely tightened.

Floor

The floor is attached to the structure with screws—the outer edges of the floor are supported under the side panels. The flooring should occasionally be taken up and any dust and dirt removed.

Windows

The cabin windows are of two-piece design. Non-shatter glass being used throughout. The windows operate in a felt sealed channel which permits sliding them back or forth. In case of replacement of the glass the finish moulding on the inside of the cabin must be removed. The glass complete with felt channels can then be removed.

The cockpit enclosure is of the same general construction and the same procedure applies. The handle and seal strip are cemented to the window glass with sodium silicate.

Doors

All doors on the fuselage can be removed by withdrawing the hinge pins. The locks on the doors are standard and easily serviced. The cabin door is equipped with a safety lock on the inside of the cabin. Occasionally lubricate by placing a few drops of oil on the hinges and locks.

WING CENTER SECTION

Fuel Tanks

The fuel tanks are installed in the wing center section. They are supported in cradles and retained by supporting straps which are held together with a turnbuckle.

After considerable flying in regions of excessive humidity, replacement of the padding between the straps and the fuel tanks may be necessary. New packing should be glued to the tank with a suitable metal cement.

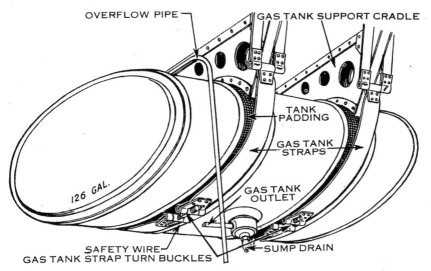

Figure 15

The tanks must be kept securely anchored at all times as one loose cradle strap will cause a tank to vibrate and eventually crack the welded joints.

Replacing of the padding between the straps and fuel tanks (see Fig. 15), can be done either inside of the wing or by completely removing the tanks. The tanks are removed from the wing as follows:

Drain the gasoline by opening plug on the tank sump. This plug can be reached through the inspection door on the under side of the wing beneath the tanks. Loosen the hose clamps at the rubber connections and disconnect the fuel lines at the tanks. The ceiling in the cabin

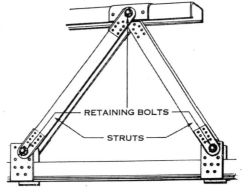

Figure 16

between spar No. 1 and No. 2 and the tie rods above ceiling must also be removed. (See Fig. 8). The wing structure located on either side of the ceiling opening can be removed by withdrawing the retaining bolts. (See Fig. 16). This allows convenient access to the fuel tanks.

The turnbuckles on the bottom of the tanks are then loosened, the sump cock removed and the tanks dropped free of the cradle. Care must be taken to replace the metal inner liners when reassembling the fuel lines.

The fuel filler on top of the wing is covered with a rubber cover. This cap must always be snug in place before making a flight.

Wing Hold Down Bolts

The fuselage is held to the wing by means of six special bolts which extend through the spar chord. These bolts and their fittings require the usual flight check inspection.

Wing Drag Bracing

The wing drag bracing is located in the wing center section between spars No. 1 and No. 3. These tie rods will require the usual flight check inspection. The tie rods should be adjusted to a uniform tension by tightening them until just snug. At points of contact the rods must be taped tightly to prevent wear.

Baggage Compartment

The baggage compartment is located between spars No. 2 and 3 on each side of the cabin. Care must be taken not to crush the cable housing. The maximum baggage load allowable is 400 pounds on each side.

Note: When removing baggage, do not rest the baggage on the backs of the passenger chairs.

Fittings

As a safety measure, inspection of the structure at all fittings is recommended. These points are: wing to fuselage fittings; motor mount to wing fittings, and the motor mount side brace fittings.

WING TIP

Ailerons

The ailerons are hinged on the wing with self aligning ball bearing type hinges. These hinges require flight inspection and occasional lubrication. A good grade of grease or heavy oil should be used for this

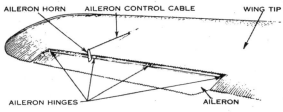

Figure 17

purpose. The bearings at the ends of the horns should also be lubricated with a good grade of oil.

Fittings

Points for flight check inspection on the wing tip structure are the tip to center section fittings and pins, and the aileron hinges. The wing hinge pins are inspected by loosening the turn buckles on the straps covering the gap between the wing center section and wing tip, then sliding the strap to one side. The hinge pins should be cottered and safety wired.

TAIL SURFACES

Stabilizer Brace

The front stabilizer beam is braced with diagonal tubes which extend to the lower side of·the fuselage. At the stabilizer end the strut is fitted with a ball socket joint which will require occasional lubrication. There is no need to change the adjustment at the end of the strut as this adjustment is intended for manufacturing purposes only.

At the fuselage end, the stabilizer brace tube is bolted to a bulkhead fitting (see Fig. 18). In addition to the brace, a drag wire is run from the fuselage to the ball joint of the brace tube.

Fin

The vertical fin is bolted to the fuselage tail post and to a vertical fitting on the fuselage decking. Two wires serve as an additional brace. These wires run from the top of the fin into the horizontal stabilizer. The wires should be kept snug but not tight enough to cause excessive loads on the structure. No servicing of this part is necessary beyond the usual flight inspection.

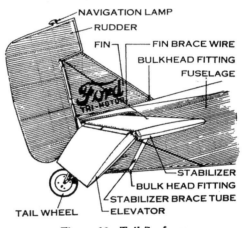

Figure 18—Tail Surfaces

Rudder

The rudder is mounted on hinges on the fin post (see Fig. 12). These hinges are of the self aligning ball type. To lubricate, place a little grease or heavy oil on the hinge bearings, also oil the end of the horn, where the cable is attached. The rudder will require the usual flight inspection.

Elevator

The elevator is mounted on self-aligning, ball-bearing hinges which are attached to the horizontal stabilizer. Since the two halves of the elevator work independently of each other, they should be properly aligned to insure minimum drag. Elevators must be assembled according to "TOP" and "BOTTOM" markings on the horns. The elevator and hinges require the same inspection as the rudder and hinges.

AXLE TUBE ASSEMBLY

This assembly also includes the wheel brakes. . The brakes will be treated separately.

At its lower end the axle tube is sweated and bolted into the wheel spindle. The axle collar fitting is attached to the shock absorber strut and rear brace. Between the wheel and the collar fitting the brake beam castings swing free on the wheel spindle. (See Fig. 19).

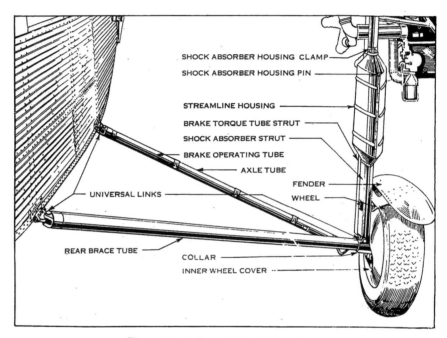

SHOCK ABSORBER HOUSING CLAMP
SHOCK ABSORBER HOUSING PIN

STREAMLINE HOUSING
BRAKE TORQUE TUBE STRUT
SHOCK ABSORBER STRUT
BRAKE OPERATING TUBE
AXLE TUBE
FENDER
UNIVERSAL LINKS
WHEEL

REAR BRACE TUBE
COLLAR
INNER WHEEL COVER

Figure 19—Axle and Shock Absorber

TERMINAL JOINTS

At the fuselage end, the axle tube is fitted in the same manner as the rear brace.

Lubrication of the universal link is the only servicing required at this point.

SHOCK ABSORBER UNITS

The shock absorber unit is a telescoping tube employing rubber compression discs to absorb shocks of landing (see Fig. 20). The rebound of the rubbers is checked by the rubbers themselves through cables and sliding washers. The rubbers may require replacement under severe weather conditions. No additional service of this unit is required other than occasional lubrication of the telescopic tubes:

WHEEL ASSEMBLY

The wheel is mounted on tapered roller bearings, and may be lubricated with grease or a heavy oil, through a pressure lubricator connection. Access to the lubricator connection is made through the hole in the outer wheel disc.

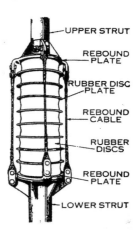

UPPER STRUT

REBOUND PLATE

RUBBER DISC PLATE

REBOUND CABLE

RUBBER DISCS

REBOUND PLATE

LOWER STRUT

Figure 20
Shock Absorber Unit

REMOVAL OF WHEEL

To remove a wheel for inspection, it is first necessary to remove the fender assembly; second, the inner and outer wheel covers; third, remove the brake shoes from brake beam assembly. The felt oil seal and its retainer washer can then be withdrawn from the hub.

The adjustment nut and the spindle nut are now accessible. Before unscrewing the nut, the large cotter pin must be removed. (Note that the right-hand axle spindle is threaded left hand and the left hand spindle has right-hand threads. This prevents any possibility of crowding the bearings.) Unscrew this outer spindle nut and slide off adjustment lock washer. The bearing adjustment nut is next removed. The wheel can now be pulled off the spindle bearing, care being taken to catch the outer bearing cone as the wheel comes off. After removal of the wheel, the inner bearing cone, the inner oil seal, and the brake beam assembly are exposed. (See Fig. 21).

Wheel Inspection

The wheel should be inspected for loose spokes and brake drum wear. If any spokes are loose care should be taken *not* to pull the rim out of line with the hub when tightening. If possible, the V-drum should be checked with a micrometer gauge to within .005 of an inch by spinning the wheel on the bearings and spindle, after drawing up the spokes.

The wheels should be jacked up periodically and tested for smoothness of running and excessive side play. To check side play, grasp the sides of the tire and shake the wheel. If wheels are loose adjust bearings.

Bearing Adjustment

To adjust the wheel bearings, proceed as follows:

The wheel spindle is assumed bare without bearing cones or brake beam. The entire wheel spindle from the landing gear collar to the threaded end should be greased with heavy oil or high grade cup grease. The brake beam is mounted next to the collar with the ball anchor stud to the front and the hose fitting to the inside. It should be a free running fit, allowing the beam to rock easily, with no tendency to bind. The brake beam spacer is a "Z" section washer which is fitted to the remaining portion of the large diameter section of the spindle.

The felt oil seal and its retaining washers may be ignored, since correction for their drag cannot be made during bearing adjustment.

The large cone is next passed over the spindle, large end first, and backed against the brake beam spacer bushing (see Fig. 21). It should be a loose fit on the spindle to permit cone creep.

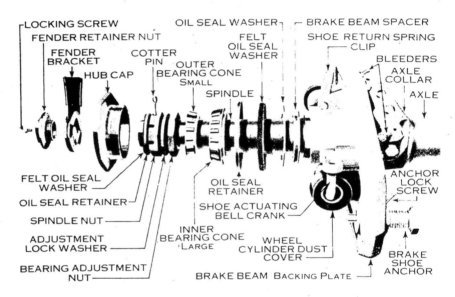

Figure 21—Wheel Spindle Assembly

The wheel is placed on the spindle and bearing cone (it is assumed that the bearing cups are already pressed into place in the wheel hub). The small bearing cone is next passed over the spindle, small end first, and fitted into its cup.

The assembly is now ready for the adjusting nuts. The adjusting nut is the large check nut with the two projecting pins. It is screwed onto the spindle in the direction opposite to normal wheel rotation. The pins must be to the outside. This nut is drawn up until there is a tendency for the bearing to drag. It is then backed off about one-quarter turn, which allows the wheel to spin freely and provides from .002 to .005 of an inch end play. The position of the nut should now be marked so that it may be relocated to the correct adjustment position.

To assemble the oil seal enclosures, the entire wheel and bearing assembly up to the brake beam spacer, is removed. The flat steel washer, the felt washer, and the cupped retainer washer flanged over the felt are assembled on the spacer bushing in the order named. The large bearing cone is again mounted and the assembly proceeds as above until the bearing adjustment nut (see Fig. 21), has been relocated in its marked position.

The wheel should be spun to check the adjustment, fair allowance being made for enclosure drag. The adjustment lock washer is fitted to the threaded spindle end. The pins of the adjusting nut lock into the holes in the washer. In case they do not match positions, the bearing adjusting nut should be drawn off to the nearest hole, providing the increase in end play is not critical. The castellated spindle nut is next screwed tightly against the lock washer and locked with a spring cotter key. The outer oil seal retainer washer is placed on the spindle flange toward the outside and the small felt seal washer is inserted. Then reassemble brake shoes. This completes the internal hub assembly. Snap the outer wheel cover disc onto the wheel rim and clamp it at the hub by screwing on the large cast hub cap. The fender bracket fitting is mounted on the remaining shaft and the spindle end cap screwed on and locked. The hub should now be filled with lubricant.

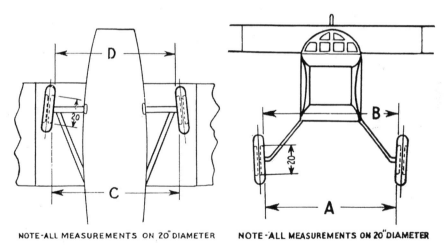

NOTE-ALL MEASUREMENTS ON 20" DIAMETER   NOTE-ALL MEASUREMENTS ON 20" DIAMETER

Figure 22   Toe-in and Camber   Figure 23

Toe-in and Camber

Figs. 22 and 23 show the points at which the toe-in and camber can be checked. The correct toe-in in the flying position is 0 to $\frac{1}{1}$", in other words C minus D (Fig. 22) should equal 0 to $\frac{1}{1}$". In the landing position, the maximum toe-in should not exceed 1".

The maximum camber is $\frac{3}{4}''$ in the flying position (B minus A equals $\frac{3}{4}''$, see Fig. 23). The camber is not adjustable, as it is provided for in the forging of the axle.

Dimensions C-D and A-B are to be taken on the 20'' diameter flange of the rim. (See Figs. 22 and 23.)

Placing the fork in the forward position gives the maximum toe-in. Placing the fork in the rear position gives the minimum toe-in. (See Figs. 23 and 24.)

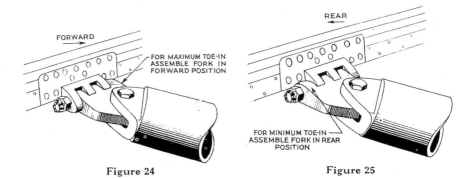

REAR

FORWARD

FOR MAXIMUM TOE-IN
ASSEMBLE FORK IN
FORWARD POSITION

FOR MINIMUM TOE-IN
ASSEMBLE FORK IN REAR
POSITION

Figure 24   Figure 25

Removing Tires

To remove tire from rim, remove valve cap and lock nut, and place wheel so that valve is at the top. Let all air out of tube. Push valve stem up into tire. Working both ways from the valve, press the tire together and down in to the rim well, approximately two feet each side of the valve stem. Insert tire iron under bead at point opposite valve and force bead over rim. The tire can then be removed from the rim with the hands. Do not attempt to force both beads over the rim at the same time. If a tire iron is used, care must be exercised not to damage the soft feather edge on the inner edge of the bead.

Mounting Tires

Inflate tube until it is barely rounded out, and insert tube into casing (caution: never use a tire flap when mounting tires). With wheel placed so that valve stem hole is at top. Next place casing and tube on wheel. With valve in valve stem hole. Next press the casing together and down into the rim well, until lower part of casing can be forced over rim flange at bottom. *Before inflating,* raise tire up, work casing back and forth until beads are seated on bead seats and tire is properly centered on rim.

It is particularly important that the tire seats on the bead seat on both sides before fully inflating tire. Place valve nut over valve stem and draw nut down tightly against rim, inflate tires to 55 pounds on 4 AT Models, and 60 pounds on 5 AT Models. Keep both tires equally inflated at all times to insure equal surface contact. After inflating tires to proper air pressure screw the valve cap down tightly over end of valve stem. This is important as a tight application of the valve cap prevents any air leakage at the valve stem. The tail wheel tire should be inflated to 50 pounds.

Due to the use of brakes, the tires are subjected to considerable wear and possibly some cutting, depending upon the nature of the landing field surfaces. To get the most service, tires should be frequently inspected and all cuts or holes properly sealed or repaired. This prevents dirt and water working in between the rubber and fabric and causing blisters or sand holes. If the airplane is laid up for several months, it is advisable to remove the tires. Wrap up the outer casings and inner tubes separately, and store in a cool dark room. Oil or grease can be removed from the tires with gasoline.

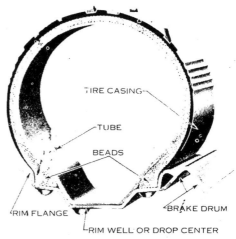

Figure 26 Sectional View of Tire and Rim

BRAKE TENSION TUBE

At its upper end the brake tension tube is attached to the engine mount ring through a universal joint. This joint should be well lubricated. At the lower end of the strut is an adjustable ball joint which is a free fit on the ball anchor stud on the brake beam (see Fig. 27). Adjustment is made through the screw plug in the end. This plug should be securely locked and the joint packed with grease. No accessories should be attached to the strut since its movement is not regular and weights may cause excessive vibration in the air.

FENDER ASSEMBLY

The fender is attached at the shock absorber strut and at the outer axle spindle. There are no points of lubrication. To remove, take out the bolts at the shock absorber strut fitting and remove the spindle cap nut.

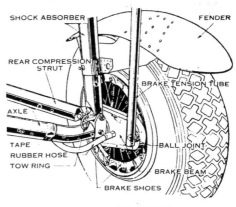

Figure 27—Wheel Unit

HYDRAULIC BRAKE SYSTEM

In as much as brakes are a comparatively new service item for airplane mechanics, detailed service and inspection instructions covering the Ford Servo-Hydraulic Brake System are given.

How the Brakes Operate

When the brake lever is pulled straight back the brakes are applied to both wheels.

When the brake lever is pulled back at approximately a 45° angle to the left, the brake is applied to the left wheel.

When the lever is pulled back at approximately a 45° angle to the right the brake is applied to the right wheel. (See Fig. 28).

Description of Brakes

Each wheel is equipped with a "V" drum integral with the rim. Holes are drilled into the bottom of the "V" in order to prevent the accumulation of dirt, water, etc. The inside of the "V" is ground to within .003"of specified dimensions. Inside of the drum are four brake shoes (see Fig. 29). Their cross-section permits the special brake lining to act on both sides of the "V" drum. The lining is prepared with a pre-determined co-efficient of friction and is of a special woven shape to fit the conical surface of the brake shoe.

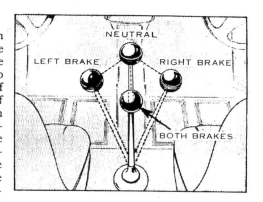

Figure 28 Brake Lever Positions

Stock for relining should be ordered only through the Airplane division of the Ford Motor Company. When relining the shoes, the old sections of lining should be used as a template for drilling the rivet holes in the new lining. The split end brass rivets which hold the lining to the shoe are clinched into the lining. The shoes are mounted on the brake beam in pairs and it should be noted that the anchored shoe is not lined for its full length but only to within four inches of the anchor end. The actuated shoe is lined full length. To prevent the lining crowding into the "V" drum it is important that the outer edge of the lining be flush with the outer edge of the brake shoe "V".

Brake Shoe Adjustment

Occasional adjustment of the brake shoes will be necessary to compensate for brake lining wear. When performing this operation, block one of the wheels to prevent its rolling, then jack up the other wheel free of the ground. The jack should be placed under the axle tube collar fitting. Next remove the inner wheel covers. At the actuated end of the brake shoe assembly there is a threaded push rod and adjustment ball nut which is locked with a check nut. After loosening the check nut spin the wheel, then turn the ball nut until a drag is felt on the wheel. Next loosen the adjustment nut until the wheel just turns free. It will be found that this adjustment provides ABOUT ¹⁄₃₂" CLEARANCE NEAR THE ANCHOR SHOE AND ¹⁄₁₆"CLEARANCE AT THE BELL CRANK SHOE. After making the adjustment set the check nut against

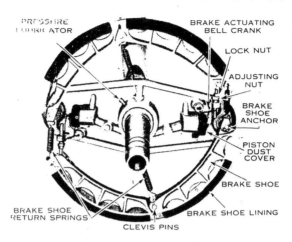

Figure 29— Brake Shoes

the adjustment nut and replace the covers. The shoes of the opposite wheel should now be adjusted as it is always advisable to adjust both wheels when making brake adjustments.

Removal of Brake Shoes

It is necessary to remove the outer and inner wheel discs to disassemble the brake shoes. To perform this operation remove the outer wheel disc by unscrewing the spindle cap and sliding off the fender bracket. Next remove the hub cap and the wheel disc. The brake shoe adjustment nuts at the actuated end of the brake shoe assembly are next loosened, relieving the tension in the brake shoe return springs. Working from the outside of the wheel through the spokes, the cotter pins in the front and rear anchor studs are withdrawn.

When the mechanic becomes sufficiently acquainted with the wheel brake system it is possible to remove these cotter pins from the inside of the wheel. This requires only the removal of the inside wheel covers. Withdrawing the cotter pins makes it possible to release the set screw lock in the anchor studs and to screw them far enough out of the beam to free the brake shoe assemblies with their springs. The springs are unhooked from their clips and the shoes in pairs are drawn out through the inside of the wheel between the beam and the brake drum. All joints at the ends of the brake shoes should be free and well lubricated with graphited grease. Clevis pins at these points furnish a constant clearance.

The brake shoe return springs should be elastic at all times and should be replaced once they lose their elasticity. With the shoes removed the brake bell crank can be inspected for clearance. Sufficient clearance has been provided so that with occasional lubrication no binding should occur. A pressure lubricator connection is provided on the brake beam to lubricate the surface between the axle spindle and the brake beam.

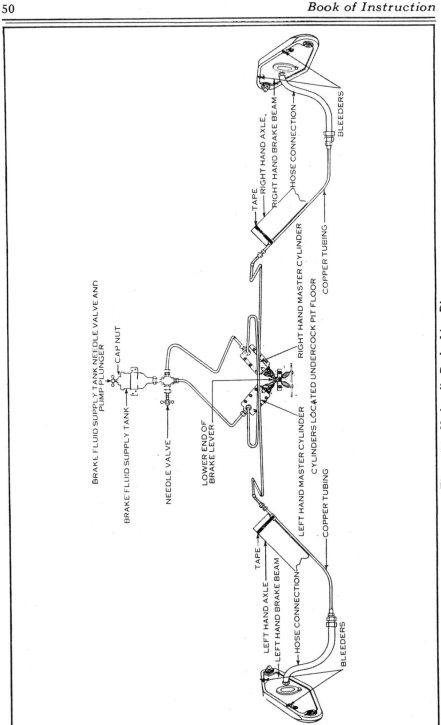

Figure 30—Hydraulic Brake Line Diagram

This completes the mechanical features of the wheel brakes. The Hydraulic system will now be described.

Wheel Pistons

Two cylinders are cast on the brake beam. These cylinders contain a piston and a piston cup, and are sealed with a rubber dust cover. The piston cup is moulded from special rubber and is clipped to the die-cast piston. To prevent leakage it is important that the edge of the rubber cup be sharp and the surface of the cup and piston free from scratches. The cylinder walls should be inspected for scores.

Hydraulic Lines

Holes are drilled in the casting from the cylinders to the brake beam inlet fitting. This fitting is a hollow bolt which takes the flexible rubber hose from the axle tube. This bolt is screwed through the beam and sealed with a copper washer and an acorn nut. It is set with a mixture of litharge (litharge is a combination of lead oxide and glycerine). The flexible rubber hose end is threaded and sweated into the inlet bolt and leads to a union fitting on the axle tube connecting with the hydraulic line. This line is constructed of ¼″ copper tubing. The rubber hose is of the standard Lockheed brake type. The copper hydraulic line is taped to the axle tube and connects at its upper end to the fuselage line, which leads to the master brake cylinder below the cockpit floor. This cylinder contains a rubber piston cup and a die-cast piston with a ball-socket piston rod (the same rules of scores and scratches apply here as at the wheel cylinder). From the upper part of this cylinder a hydraulic line leads to the system supply pump behind the pilot's seat. (See Fig. 30.)

The entire system is duplicated for the opposite wheel, there being two independent hydraulic systems with the pump common to both. The supply pump serves both as a reservoir and a pump when forcing hydraulic fluid into the system in case of minor leaks.

Master Cylinder

The master cylinder piston rod receives the sliding push rod of the brake control lever. (On some types a stop is provided in the form of a locknut, on other types a compression spring transmits the brake lever pressure.) This sliding joint must remain free so that the master cylinder piston cup is not pulled back by the brake lever but is returned by the hydraulic pressure in the lines. This prevents the drawing in of air.

The tank should be kept to the three-quarter level. STANDARD LOCKHEED BRAKE FLUID OR A 50% ALCOHOL AND 50% CASTOR OIL MIXTURE MUST BE USED IN THE HYDRAULIC SYSTEM. MINERAL OILS, GASOLINE, GLYCERINE, AND OTHER SUBSTANCES CAUSE THE RUBBER CUPS TO SWELL AND CORRECT BRAKE OPERATION CEASES. THIS POINT IS VERY IMPORTANT. IF ANY BRAKE PARTS REQUIRE CLEANING, THEY SHOULD BE CLEANED IN ALCOHOL TO AVOID INTRODUCTION OF ANY DAMAGING SUBSTANCE.

CONNECTING HYDRAULIC BRAKE ASSEMBLY

The tubing projecting from the fuselage below the axle fitting is connected to the copper tube on the axle through the union fitting attached thereto. The axle tube is then covered with its fairing. The system is now ready for filling and bleeding. The two bleeder screws are located at the front and rear of the upper flange of the brake beam.

The $\frac{3}{16}$ machine screw and lock washer is removed and two sections of $\frac{3}{16}''$ rubber tubes about 12" long are slipped over the projecting nipples. The bleeder fittings are now unscrewed about four turns in order to release the needle valve in the beam. Both front and rear bleeders are now open and the system is ready to fill.

The supply pump is located behind the pilot's seat in the pilot's compartment, on the right side of the fuselage. The handle of this tank should be unscrewed until it is possible to pump it (about 20 turns is necessary), On the bottom of this tank is another needle valve which should also be unscrewed when filling the brake lines with fluid. (See Fig. 31.)

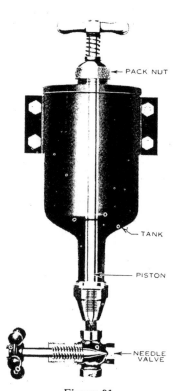

Figure 31
Hydraulic Fluid Supply Tank

The pack nut is next unscrewed and the piston removed from the tank. The tank is then filled with hydraulic fluid which drains through the system, forcing all air from the lines. The rubber tubes at the brake beam must lead into a clean open top container, a glass jar can be used for this purpose (see Fig. 32). The supply tank must be kept full throughout the bleeder operations. When the flow of fluid from the bleeder is free from air bubbles, the beam is tipped so that the opposite end is higher. The flow is allowed to continue until it is free from air bubbles. There can be no compromise in bleeding the hydraulic system; all trace of air in the tubes must have disappeared. At least one pint of fluid must be allowed to drain clear after the appearance of the last air bubble to insure a complete passage of liquid from supply tank to brake beam. The easiest method to obtain best results is by rocking the beam to prevent air trapping. The brake lever should not be applied while bleeding or pumping.

When the flow from both bleeders is free of air, the bleeder fittings must be screwed tight into the beam, the needle valve seated, the rubber hose removed and the machine screw and lock washer replaced. The supply tank must be at least three-quarters full. The piston assembly is replaced in the tank and the knurled pack nut tightened. The system can now be pumped full of liquid. The supply pump should be pumped until the brake control lever moves at every pump stroke. This pumping is not intended to build up a pressure in the hydraulic system, but merely insures a system completely filled with fluid. The pump and needle valve handles are then screwed down until the needle valves are seated.

Servicing Brake System

In case the action of the brake control lever indicates a "soft" system, pumping up the system or bleeding may remedy the trouble. A partially empty system which requires pumping can be recognized by the fact that considerable movement of the brake lever is required before any resistance

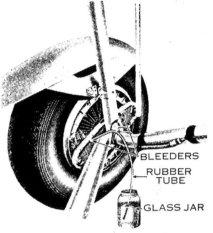

Figure 32—Bleeding Operation

is felt or any brake action starts, also the lever appears to be free and is not self-centering. To pump up the system unscrew the handle of the supply pump and the needle valve. About 20 turns are necessary to release the needle valve in the supply tank. The handle may now be pumped until the system is full, which condition is recognized by the movement of the control lever with each stroke of the pump. The handle is next screwed into the pump again and the needle valve seated.

Bleeding the system will free the hydraulic lines and cylinders of any air which has been trapped and will give correct hydraulic action.

CAUTIONS REGARDING FORD SERVO-HYDRAULIC BRAKES

1. Watch the brake shoe adjustment and keep the clearance within the recommended limits.

2. Inspect hydraulic lines and promptly repair leaks when found.

3. Do not alter location of hydraulic lines. They have been installed with particular regard to prevention of conditions causing air trapping.

4. Air is compressible and should be removed from any hydraulic system. Bleed the systems if there are any indications of air.

5. Use only the specified fluid in the brake systems. Even small percentages of impurities will damage the system.

6. Keep the needle valve of the supply pump tightly closed. **Unless this valve is kept tightly closed, it will be impossible to build up hydraulic pressure on the brakes.** The supply reservoir should be kept from half to three-quarters full at all times to prevent churning and introduction of air bubbles when pumping.

7. Moisture will affect the coefficient of friction of brake lining. The wheel cover discs must therefore be kept in place and closely fitted to insure dry braking surfaces.

   Brakes are placed on an airplane to act as a safety device to make landings in short fields and quick stopping possible in case of emergency. They should not be used unless absolutely necessary.

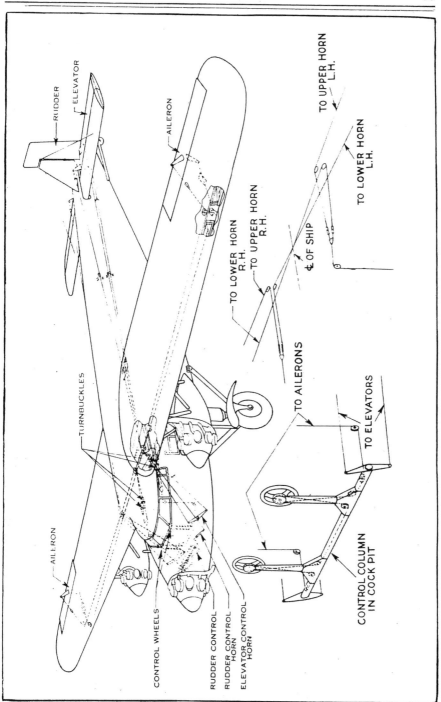

Figure 33· Surface Controls· Model 5–AT·· Below Plane No. 45

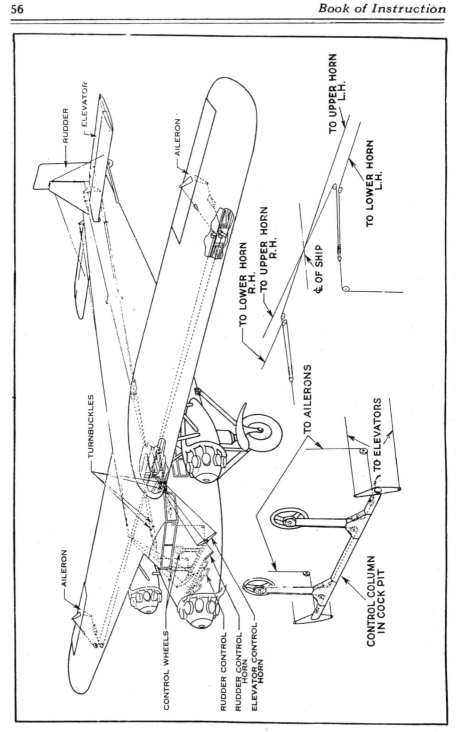

Figure 34—Surface Controls on Model 5-AT—Above Plane No. 45

SURFACE CONTROLS

THE surface controls on the Ford all-metal monoplane include the dual control wheels for elevators and ailerons, the dual rudder control, operated through pedal stirrups, and the stabilizer adjustment.

Control Column

The dual control column unit is mounted in two large bearings, on the floor of the pilot's compartment. The two columns are connected by a cross tube passing through the sides of the ship and carrying the master elevator control horns. The cross tube bearings should be kept well lubricated. Lubricator fittings are provided for this purpose. At the top of the column the three-spoke control wheel is bolted to a short shaft and drum that revolves on ball bearings. The bearings are enclosed in a casting which is drilled for oil holes. The wheel is held in place by four bolts. The wheel should be mounted so that the trade-marked spoke is vertical with the ailerons neutral.

Aileron Adjustment

Adjustment of cable lengths for proper alignment of ailerons is made at the turnbuckles found inside the front compartment housing. The cables lead directly off the aileron horns and pass through leather fair-leads into the wing, then to the front spar where pulleys are mounted. The pulleys are mounted on self-lubricating bearings and require no additional lubrication. For correct alignment, the bottom of the aileron and wing should be in a straight line at the inboard end of the aileron.

Elevator Cables

The elevator control horns are mounted on both sides of the fuselage at the projecting ends of the control column cross tube. Cables lead from these horns through the lower wing surface and over pulleys on the center wing spar (see Fig. 13). They then pass through the upper surface of the wing and through fairleads along the fuselage to the turnbuckles at the elevator horns. Adjustment for correct length is made at this point. Pulleys used in the elevator control system are provided with ball bearings. The bearings should occasionally be lubricated with a good grade of grease or heavy oil.

Rudder Control

The rudder control in the pilot's compartment consists of two cross tubes mounted in self-aligning bearings on the motor bulkhead and four tubular pedal stirrups. The cross tubes are geared together through spur gears which provide a stop as well as the elimination of a tension control system. The removable pedal housings allow full pedal movement and provide ample foot room. The gear box is packed with grease. The grease requires renewal every year. The universal bearing at the side requires no attention. The rudder control cables lead from the single horn on the rudder cross tube, through the wing and along the fuselage to the rudder, in the same manner as the elevator control cables. Length adjustment is made by means of a turnbuckle at the rudder horn. Pulleys used in the rudder control system are provided with ball bearings. These bearings should occasionally be lubricated with a good grade of grease or heavy oil.

Removing Rudder Pedals

In case it is necessary to disassemble the rudder control pedals, the cowling and oil tank must be removed to allow the pedal housings to be detached from the bulkhead. The bearing caps at the sides of the bulkhead are then removed and the gear box at the center uncovered. This permits the pedal and cross tube assembly to be lifted out. All alignment adjustments are set at the factory and need not be altered when removing the pedals.

Stabilizer Adjustment

The stabilizer adjustment crank is located above the pilot's compartment entrance between the two seats. It is connected by sprocket and chain to a shaft inside the cabin, which runs along the fuselage side to the tail of the ship (see Fig. 35). It is supported by self-aligning, oilless bearings and fabric universal joints. The end of the shaft is connected to the stabilizer adjustment screw which is bolted to the fuselage tail post.

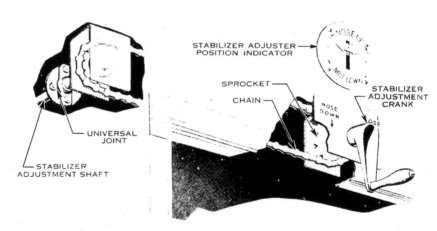

Figure 35—Stabilizer Adjuster in Pilot's Compartment

Stabilizer Indicator

The stabilizer indicator indicates the position of the stabilizer. The indicator is mounted directly above the stabilizer adjuster handle and operates on a screw thread on the shaft of the stabilizer adjuster.

The indicator requires no service beyond occasional lubrication.

Stabilizer Adjustment Screw

The stabilizer adjustment screw (see Fig. 36) is a separate unit consisting of a worm gear combined with a double thread screw. The unit is oil-sealed and leaves the factory with sufficient lubricant to last for some time. It should, however, be inspected occasionally and more lubricant added when necessary. To remove the unit, disconnect the drive shaft universal, release the stabilizer connecting link by withdrawing one bolt, and removing the four bolts on the tail post. Access can be had through the inspection door at the rear of the fuselage. The fabric universal joints should be inspected in those regions where climatic conditions influence such materials. Should binding occur, a systematic inspection should be made of the entire adjustment mechanism, as well as the stabilizer hinges and braces. Breaking the connection between the stabilizer and the adjustment unit will determine whether this trouble is in the stabilizer or in the adjustment. Disconnecting the universal joint at the adjustment screws will isolate the binding in either the shaft or the screw unit. The grease in this unit is a special cold test grease and should be replaced with the same kind only —freezing of the unit may be experienced if inferior grease is used. During cold weather the bottom of the stabilizer adjustment should be taken off occasionally and all condensation carefully removed.

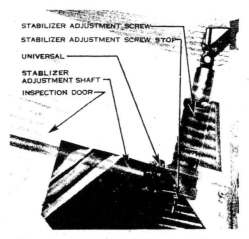

STABILIZER ADJUSTMENT SCREW
STABILIZER ADJUSTMENT SCREW STOP
UNIVERSAL
STABILIZER ADJUSTMENT SHAFT
INSPECTION DOOR

Figure 36—Stabilizer Adjustment Screw

TAIL WHEEL

The tail wheel consists of a shock absorber enclosed in a cloth cover, a tension fork, a wheel and tire (see Fig. 14). The shock absorber unit is a telescoping tube employing rubber compression discs to absorb shocks of landing. It is similar in construction to the landing gear shock absorber described on page 43. No service of this unit is required other than occasional lubrication of the telescopic tubes and of the swivel bolts on the tail post. These bolts are provided with pressure lubricators. Sufficient clearance must be maintained to prevent the bolts binding.

The tension fork is a welded steel tube fork. It requires no servicing. The wheel is mounted on bronze bearings which will require occasional lubrication. Two shock cords are stretched between the radius fork and the lower stabilizer brace fitting to properly trail the wheel.

For mounting and removing tire, see page 46.

ENGINE CONTROLS

Each engine has two running controls, namely, throttle and altitude. Their control levers are fitted in the pilot's compartment on a control knee placed between the pilot seats. The throttle control is mounted on top of the knee, the altitude control is at the front. Both lever assemblies are of the friction type equipped with an adjustable friction spring.

A bell crank and push rod system connects the controls in the pilot's compartment to the engines. Both the bell crank and push rod shafts are mounted on self-aligning ball bearings which require a few drops of oil from time to time. The same applies to the clevis pins at the joints of the bell cranks and push rods.

Engine Cowling

The center and outboard engine assemblies are completely cowled with removable sheet aluminum cowling. Support rings are bolted to the engines and engine mounts and are provided with anchor pins to receive the grommetted holes in the cowling. An opening has been left in the forepart of the cowling to provide for crankcase cooling and cowling ventilation. Louvres at the rear facilitate air flow and may be closed in cold weather when cooling is not desired. The sections of cowling between the engine cylinders are removable for servicing of the magnetos and ignition systems. Standard cowling safety pins are used on all cowlings.

FIRE EXTINGUISHERS

All planes are equipped with two fire extinguishers, one mounted just inside the cabin door, making it easily accessible from either inside or outside the ship; the other is attached to the floor behind the pilot's seat. These extinguishers should be serviced according to instructions on the name plate.

REPAIRING SKIN

Should the corrugated covering of the plane become damaged through rough usage, it is possible to restore the corrugations by bumping out the metal. Whenever the skin is damaged, it should be immediately repaired. When replacing any part of the skin, be sure to replace the same amount of rivets of the same size that were removed. Should any rivets become loose, they should be replaced with rivets of the next larger size.

If any structural members are damaged, they should immediately be repaired or reinforced. When a member is being reinforced, care must be taken not to weaken it by drilling rivet holes in line, thereby reducing the tension area.

ALUMINUM ALLOY

The alloy of aluminum used in the manufacture of the Ford all-metal planes is in the wrought state and consists mainly of aluminum with small but essential percentages of copper, magnesium, and manganese. The chemical specification for this alloy is:

Copper................ 3.5 to 4.5%
Manganese............ 0.4 to 1.0%
Magnesium........... 0.2 to 0.75%
Aluminum............92.0% Minimum

Iron is usually less than 1''. The composition may vary somewhat according to the proposed use of the alloy.

The aluminum alloy is supplied in the cold rolled state and in various tempers. If annealed or hot rolled prior to cold rolling, it is known as "Hard Wrought Temper"; if heat treated and cooled after final rolling to remove work-hardening effects, it is termed "Annealed Temper." By suitable heat treatment, the tensile strength and hardness may be considerably increased over that obtainable in the annealed state, known as "Heat Treated Temper."

Aluminum alloy is one of the comparatively few alloys susceptible to "Precipitation Hardening," and it is due to this property that it is possible to form aluminum alloy, or head up rivets made of this alloy, if done within two hours after quenching from the hardening temperature of 950° F.

By reason of the precipitation hardening which takes place, the tensile strength and hardness of the alloy rapidly increases after quenching without any outside assistance other than the temperature of the room, and stability is attained after approximately four days. The age hardening is totally inhibited at very low temperatures. This aging may also be accomplished by immersion in boiling water for several hours.

Cn samples heat treated in this way, by quenching from 950° and aging four days, the following physical properties are regularly obtained:

Yield Point . . . . 30,000 to 40,000 lbs. per sq. in.
Tensile Strength . . . . 55,000 to 65,000 lbs. per sq. in.
Elongation in 2" . . . . 18 to 25''
Brinell Hardness . . . . 90 to 105, 500Kg.

On very thin sections, due to their proportion, the elongation may be as low as 16''. Young's modulus is about 10,000,000 lbs. per sq. in. Specific gravity 2.85 maximum.

For hardening, the most satisfactory method is that of heating in a bath of fused mixed nitrates, 50'' sodium nitrate and 50% pot nitrate. This mixture is contained in a pot of heat resisting alloy and brought up to temperature by any suitable means of heating.

Heat Treatment of Aluminum Alloy

To correctly heat treat aluminum alloy stock and obtain maximum physical properties, it is vitally necessary to observe certain precautions.

1. Equipment must be of sufficient capacity and design to handle the material without losing more than 60° F. of heat. That is, at no time while working should the temperature fall below 900° F. due to heat losses in charging, etc.

2. It is necessary to maintain the temperature during heat treatment between the limits of 925° F. and 950°, with 950° F. as the preferred temperature. Aluminum alloy will not harden at temperatures below 925° F. The duration of the treatment must in all cases be counted from the time the temperature of the furnace reaches a minimum of 925° F. regardless of how long the stock has taken to reach this temperature.

3. Since aluminum alloy becomes plastic and partially melted at temperatures over 960° F., it is equally important that this temperature should not be exceeded. A common cause of excessive heat occurs where the stock is allowed to rest on the bottom of the furnace pot.

4. The most desirable condition is to have a continuous type of furnace maintained at 950° F. Failing this, the burden of the furnace must be sufficiently light to allow the furnace to maintain a minimum of 900° F. and recover to the treatment temperature of 925° F. minimum, quickly and easily. The use of a perforated metal cage, suspended from the top of the furnace and extending to not less than 2″ from the bottom of the furnace will help considerably in avoiding burned stock.

5. Since a definite weight of metal requires a definite amount of heat to raise its temperature to a required degree, it is obvious that the time required for the furnace to recover from the charge will be directly proportional to the weight of the load. It is therefore self evident that it is both bad practice and poor economy to overload the furnace when charging.

Part IV

FUEL SYSTEM

Shut-off Cocks—Strainers

Gasoline Gauges

Oil Tanks—Connections

Oiling Chart

FUEL SYSTEM

ALL three engines are supplied with gasoline from the three fuel tanks mounted in the wing center section on both sides of the fuselage. Their installation has been covered under the wing center section title. The gasoline filler cap is chained to the tank and is a simple clamped cover. The removable screen strainer in the filler neck should always be kept clean. There is an opening in the upper surface of the wing which provides access to the filler cap. Any overflow or water which may collect through the opening in the wing surface is carried off by a well, which drains through a small tube to the under surface of the wing. Each tank is provided with a drain cock. The sump is reached through a door in the lower wing surface. A tank equalizer line connects the sumps of all three tanks. The center engine and the two outboard engines are supplied directly from the two main tanks—the third tank is a reserve fuel tank controlled from the pilot's compartment. Provision has been made, however, so that by turning the gasoline valves all three engines can be run off any one tank.

Care must be taken when assembling gasoline control valves to see that the valve is in correct position with respect to markings on dial. The setting should be checked by disconnecting the gasoline line at the carburetor to make certain that the gasoline flow is as indicated on the dial.

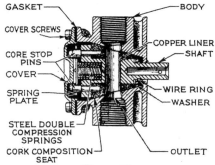

Figure 37

Fuel Control Valve

Shut-off cocks and strainers are placed in the line between tank and carburetor. The shut-off cocks for the outboard engines are remotely controlled by means of a torque rod with handles. (See Fig. 38.) The rod is located at rear just above the pilot's head. The center engine shut-off is mounted on the left side of the pilot's compartment. The center engine strainer is located ahead of the fire wall in the engine compartment. Strainers for the outboard engines are located inside the cowling of the engines. IT IS POSITIVELY NECESSARY TO DRAIN AND CLEAN STRAINERS, ALSO OPEN COCKS AT BOTTOM OF FUEL TANKS, EACH 25 HOURS OF OPERATION OR PERHAPS SOONER, DEPENDING ON THE QUALITY OF FUEL USED AND CONDITIONS SURROUNDING REFUELING. UNDER NO CIRCUMSTANCES SHOULD OPERATORS BECOME LAX IN CLEANING THE FUEL SYSTEM. Rubber hose connections are provided at all points where the fuel system passes from one structural unit to another. Replacement necessitates only the removal of two hose clamps and insertion of a new section of rubber hose. Tube liners must be used on all gasoline line rubber joints. (See Fig. 39.) All rubber joints must be replaced at least every six months.

Refueling

The plane is fueled through the upper wing surface where the fuel tank filler caps are located. Mechanics may reach the wing walkway through tne trap door in the ceiling of the front compartment. The upper surface of the wing has been reinforced between the two filler caps to permit mechanics to walk on the surface. Caution should be used, however, to step along the spars as indicated by the rows of rivets, and the painted black stripe. Access to the filler opening is obtained by removing the rubber cover, located on the wing surface, and turning the filler cap one-quarter turn.

It is advisable to shut off the tank equalizer line when filling the tanks. The filler cap strainer screen should always be in place when fueling. When the tanks have been filled, the equalizer line is again opened and the levels balanced.

Fig. 38 shows the fuel system valve controls. Figs. 39 and 40 show a layout of the fuel systems used in Models 4-AT and 5-AT planes. Fig. 41 shows gasoline gauge installation.

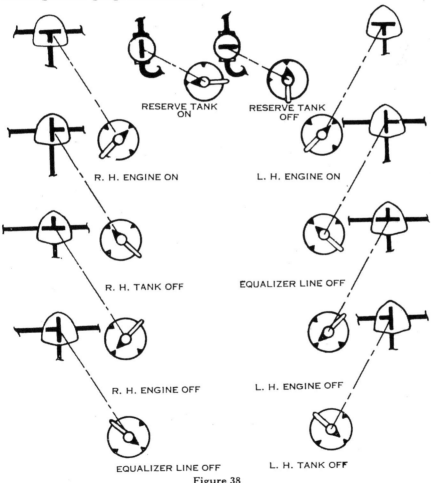

Figure 38
Fuel System Valve Controls

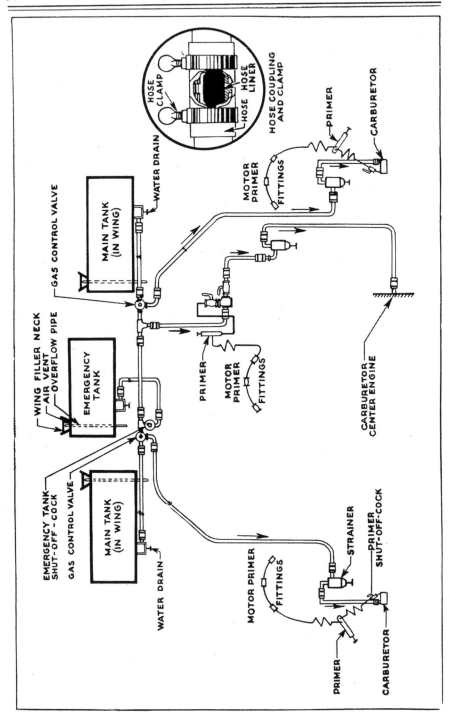

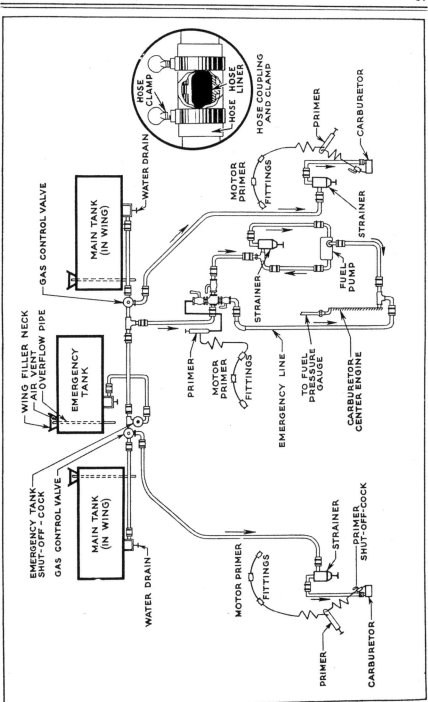

Figure 40—Fuel System Used in the Model 5-AT

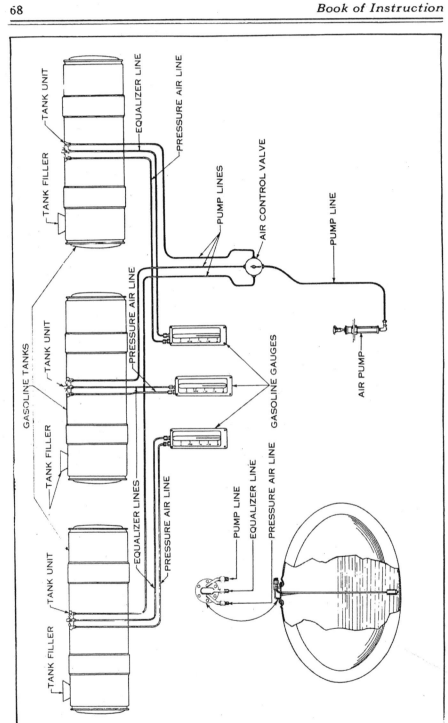

Figure 41—Gasoline Gauge Installation

GASOLINE GAUGES

Description

The gasoline gauge installation consists of four units:

1. The tank unit mounted in tanks.
2. The gauge which is mounted in the cabin. (Each tank has its individual gauge.)
3. The air lines (pressure air line, equalizer line and pump line), which run from the tank units to the recording units and pump.
4. The air pump which supplies air to the bottom of the tank units.

Operation

The tank unit consists of a hollow tube with a bell-shaped end; a small hole is provided in the bottom of the bell. The tank unit is filled with air down to the level of the hole in the bell. The gasoline in the tank presses through the hole in the bell on to the air that is entrapped in the tank unit. The more gasoline there is in the tank, the greater the pressure on the air contained in the tank unit. This pressure is transmitted from the tank unit to the gauge by means of the pressure air line which is filled with air. The gauge consists of a simple "U" tube which contains liquid. The recording leg of this U-tube is visible to the pilot. The back leg is contained within the gauge. The pressure air line is connected to the back leg of the "U" tube. The pressure transmitted from the tank unit forces the liquid down in the back leg of the "U" tube and up in the recording leg. The height that the liquid rises in the recording leg of the gauge represents the amount of gasoline in the tank.

The equalizer line, which is filled with air, connects the top of the recording leg of the gauge to the inside of the tank through the tank unit. This is to eliminate errors that would arise if there was a variation between the atmospheric pressure inside the tank and the atmospheric pressure in the cabin where the gauge is mounted.

To make certain that the tank unit is always filled with air down to level of hole in bottom of bell, the pump is mounted behind the pilot's seat. When the pump is operated, air is injected through the pump line into tank unit, filling the tank unit with air. The excess air bubbles up through the gasoline outside of the tank unit. Air must be pumped to each tank unit separately. This is accomplished by means of the air control valve, located above the window over the pilot's seat.

Before taking off, always operate air pump to verify gauge reading. The reading is correct when the liquid in the recording leg stops rising. Five strokes of the air pump for each tank unit is usually sufficient for a correction. The pump is located behind the pilot's seat near the floor.

Troubles and Repairs

1. If the gauge constantly reads too much or too little, there is either too much or not enough liquid in the gauge.

   To repair, disconnect both the pressure air line and the equalizer line at the top of the gauge. The liquid should then read exactly "0" (zero), regardless of the tank's contents.

   If the gauge reads above "0," it will be necessary to absorb the surplus liquid. An ordinary pipe cleaner can be used for this purpose. Extreme care must be exercised to prevent dirt or lint getting into the gauge.

If the gauge reads below "0," first inspect the unit to see if there is a liquid leak. If there is a leak, the unit must be replaced. If there is no leak, then add liquid through fitting where pressure air line was connected until gauge reads exactly "0." USE ONLY GENUINE KING SEELY LIQUID.

After the gauge is made to read exactly "0," reconnect both lines and operate air pump. The gauge will then record correctly.

2. If the pressure air line is disconnected, broken or leaking, no pressure will be transmitted from the tank unit to the gauge, and the gauge will always read zero when the plane is standing on the ground. Although when the plane is being flown, the gauge may register more than zero. If air line is broken or leaking, replace it.

    If either end of the pressure air line is disconnected or loosely connected, disconnect both ends and dry out air line. To dry the air line, use a hand tire pump. Push rubber hose on pump securely over tank end of air line and pump at least 50 full strokes. Then reconnect and operate air pump. The gauge will then give the correct reading.

3. If the equalizer line is disconnected, broken or leaking, the gauge will be correct only while the plane is standing on the ground. It will read zero or less while plane is being flown.

    Repairs for this condition are effected the same as under Item 2.

4. If the reading of the gauge varies badly while plane is being taxied or flown and fails to give correct reading, there is gasoline in either the pressure air line or equalizer line or in both.

    To repair, dry out both lines as described under Item 2, then reconnect and operate air pump. This will give the correct reading.

5. If liquid in the recording leg appears to be stuck and will not move up or down, it is probable that that part of the U tube which connects the back leg to the recording leg is plugged. If so, the gauge must be replaced. First, however, make the other inspections before attributing the trouble to a plugged U tube.

Replacing Units

1. To replace a gauge, proceed as follows:
    Disconnect both lines from top of gauge, and remove the gauge. Mount the new gauge in place, then remove the two nuts and cones from top of gauge. The liquid should then be made to read exactly at "0." See instructions under Repair 1. Next reconnect both lines.

2. Replacing air lines:
    Disconnect line at both ends and remove. In installing a new line, *do not let dirt or grease into the line.* Clip the line securely so it will not vibrate or chafe on some metal part of the plane.

3. Replacing a tank unit:
    First remove section of skin held in place with metal screws. This section is located just above the center of the gasoline tank. Next disconnect all lines from tank unit and remove unit by loosening the fastening screws. Next insert new unit and fasten in place. Then reconnect lines.

THE OILING SYSTEM

In the different Model planes there is a difference in the oil pipe layouts and the locations at which the various connections are made. Figures 42 to 47 show the oil pipe layouts used.

The oil supply tanks for the outboard engines are strapped to the mounts. They are welded aluminum tanks and are designed to prevent complete

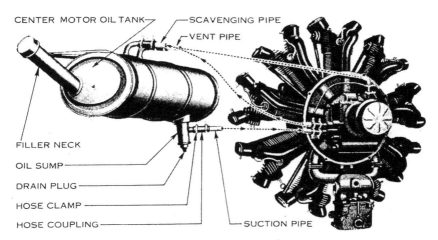

Figure 42

Oil Tank and Connections, J-5 Center Engine

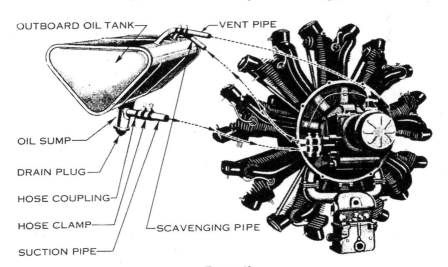

Figure 43

Oil Tank and Connections, J-5 Outboard Engine

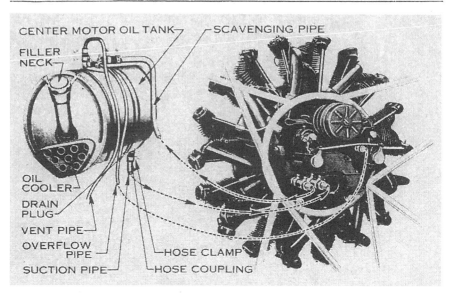

Figure 44
Oil Tank and Connections, J-6 Center Engine

filling. Two-gallon expansion space has been provided. Straps and turn-buckles form a cradle for the tanks. Felt strips are glued to the tanks for cushioning. The center engine oil supply tank is mounted on a cradle at the front fuselage bulkhead.

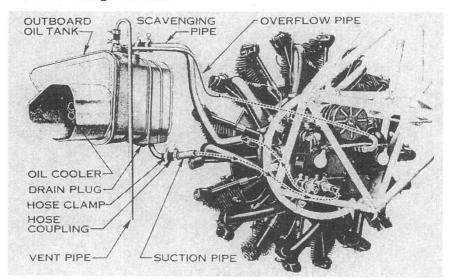

Figure 45
Oil Tank and Connections, J-6 Outboard Engine

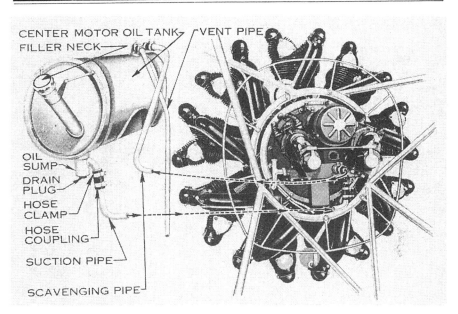

Figure 46

Oil Tank and Connections, Wasp Center Engine

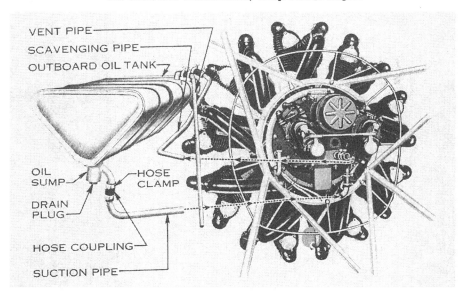

Figure 47

Oil Tank and Connections, Wasp Outboard Engine

Oil Pipes Lagged

In cold weather, depending upon the temperatures, the oil pipes between the engines and tanks should be lagged. Either large size rubber hose or flexible loom can be used for this purpose. The lag should be securely taped to the pipes. It may be necessary to install aluminum plates inside of the cowling to cover the louvres in order to obtain the desired oil temperature. When cruising, the oil outlet temperature should not be below 100° Fahrenheit.

In extremely cold weather, if the plane is going to stand a sufficient length of time to permit the oil becoming chilled, it is recommended that it be drained from each system while the oil is warm. It should then be heated and returned to the systems just before starting the engines.

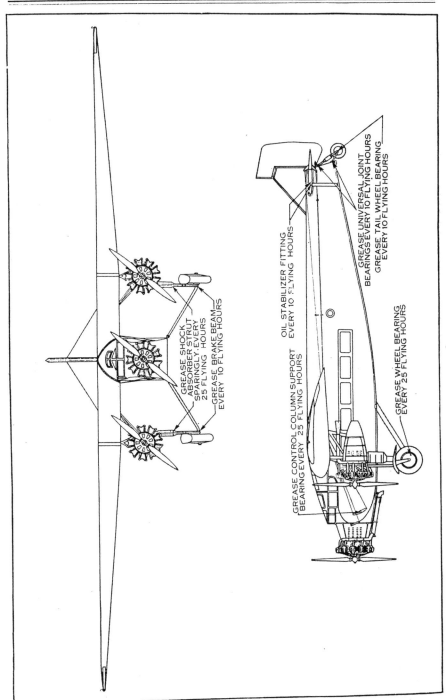

Figure 48—Oiling Chart

Part V

ELECTRICAL SYSTEM

Battery—Generator—Magnetoes, Etc.
Lighting Equipment
Wiring Diagram

ELECTRICAL SYSTEM

The Electrical System includes the following equipment:

Storage Battery
Generator (Special Equipment)
Booster Magneto
Motor Magnetos
Spark Plugs
Running Lights
Landing Lights
Volt Meter (Special Equipment)
Ammeter (Special Equipment)

The Ford System uses a twelve volt, 13 or 19 plate battery of non-spill type specially designed and built to meet the requirements of the airplane.

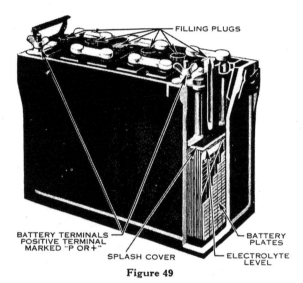

Figure 49

ADDING WATER TO BATTERY

Once a week, check the electrolyte in the battery to see that it is at the proper level. The solution (electrolyte) should be maintained level with the top of the splash cover. Do not allow the solution to enter the upper compartment, or the non-spill feature is defeated. Never cut off the filler plugs as this allows the electrolyte to escape. If the electrolyte is below the proper level, add distilled water only until the electrolyte reaches the splash cover. When adding water, the battery must be removed from the plane and placed on a level surface.

Water for battery use should be kept in clean covered vessels of glass, china, rubber or lead. In cold weather add water only immediately before charging, so that the charging will mix the water and electrolyte and prevent any possibility of freezing.

Access to the battery is easily made by removing a small door located near the floor just behind the left hand pilot seat in the cabin. To remove the battery first disconnect the cable terminals from the battery, then loosen the hold-down turnbuckles. When replacing the battery in the plane be sure to install it with the negative terminal grounded to the frame. The positive terminals are painted red-or marked "P".

Always see that the battery cover is installed before putting the plane in service.

CARE TO BE GIVEN PLUGS AND CONNECTIONS

Keep the battery filler plugs and connections tight, and the top of the battery clean. Wiping the battery with a cloth moistened with ammonia will counteract the effect of any of the solution which may have been spilt on the outside of the battery. Keep the surrounding parts and structure clean and dry at all times. Never allow soda solution or ammonia to get into cells, as these solutions neutralize the acid. If the terminals or connections show any tendency to corrode, scrape the corroded surface, then wipe them with a cloth moistened with ammonia and coat thinly with Petrolatum Jelly.

GRAVITY READINGS

The specific gravity of the electrolyte in all cells in a battery falls on discharge and rises on charge. Gravity readings indicate the state of charge of the battery. Gravity readings are taken by means of a hydrometer. Be sure to get a good instrument, cheap ones may be in error as much as 25 to 35 points. The nozzle of the Hydrometer must be long enough to reach below the splash cover. After testing, always return the electrolyte to the cell from which it was taken. The specific gravity of the electrolyte, with the cells fully charged, and with the temperature of the electrolyte approx-imately 80°F., should be between 1.285 and 1.305.

CHARGING THE BATTERY

If a battery is abnormally discharged, or if it has been operating for a considerable time with the gravity reading below 1.225 it should be given a long charge. The charging rate for the 13 plate battery is $4\frac{1}{4}$ Amperes and for the 19 plate is $6\frac{1}{2}$ Amperes or at a lower rate. Never charge at a rate that will produce a cell temperature in excess of 110°F. Only direct current must be used—never alternating current. When charging, make certain that the positive terminal of the battery is connected with the positive of the charging circuit, and the negative terminal of battery with negative of the charging circuit. If these connections are reversed the battery will be seriously damaged. Never add any special solutions to the battery. After charging the battery and before replacing it in the plane always check the level of the electrolyte. If the electrolyte is above the top of the splash plate the excess should be drawn off.

We do not recommend charging the battery in the plane when plane is not in operation.

Keep the filler plugs in the cells. Do not remove them during charge except to take specific gravity or temperature readings or to add water. The battery should be charged at least once a month.

LIGHTING EQUIPMENT

Running Lights

The running lights are arranged according to Department of Commerce regulations, that is one on each wing tip and one on the tail section. These running lights are controlled by a toggle switch located on the side of the left seat in the pilot's compartment. A 10-ampere fuse is placed in the line for protection of the wiring system.

Cabin Lights

Two styles of cabin lights are used: the 4-AT plane is equipped with two cabin dome lights and a wash room light. These lights are controlled from a switch located in the cabin near the entrance door. In addition to these lights the 5-AT plane is provided with torchier or side lights. Separate switches provide individual control for these lights. Both the cabin and instrument lights are protected with 10-ampere fuses.

Instrument Lights

There are two instrument lights located on the instrument panel in the pilot's compartment, also one instrument light on each outboard engine strut and one dome type gas gauge light in front of the cabin. These lights are controlled from a single switch on the side of the left seat in the pilot's compartment. The two pilot compartment instrument board lights have a variable resistance for controlling the amount of illumination. By turning the resistance control all the way to the left, the lights may be turned off, leaving the other lights on if desired.

Landing Lights

The landing lights are of the conventional type, mounted in the wing tip section or on the bottom of the fuselage. Each light is controlled by a separate switch, which is located along the right side of the left seat in the pilot's compartment. The 50-ampere fuses for the lights are located directly under the switches. The landing light wires are connected to a terminal panel in the wing center section over the cabin. From the connector panel each wire runs to its respective light. The single wire and ground return system is used.

Focusing Landing Lights

The lights are correctly focused and adjusted before they leave the factory. Only in cases of replacement should it be necessary to readjust or refocus them.

To focus the bulbs, direct the light upon a point about 200 feet ahead, preferably the side of a building. Next loosen the hose clamp which clamps the bulb socket in the rear of the reflector assembly, and shift the socket forward or backward until the brightest possible circle of illumination has been obtained.

When properly focused, securely tighten the hose clamp. When focusing the lights, the ship should be in the landing position.

Alignment

Alignment of the beams is made by loosening the screws which clamp the case around the spherical assembly and turning the light until the beam points in the proper direction. When alignment is completed securely, tighten the clamp screws. This will prevent any movement.

It is a good plan to occasionally clean the reflectors in the landing lights. A piece of cotton, dipped in lamp black, can be used for this purpose.

Bulbs Used

Running lights are equipped with 12-16 volt double contact 21 candlepower bulbs.

Landing lights are equipped with 12 volt 35 amp. bulbs.

Instrument lights are equipped with 12-16 volt double contact 3 candlepower bulbs.

Cabin lights are equipped with 12-16 volt double contact 8 candle power bulbs.

Ignition Switches

Ignition switches are located in the pilot's compartment. All three engines have individual switches. These same switches also control the individual magnetoes. In addition to these switches a master or emergency switch is also located in the pilot's compartment. The emergency switch controls all six magnetoes.

Ignition Wires

The wires for the center engine run directly forward from the center switch to the magneto. The outboard engine wires run from the switch to the ignition connector panel in the wing center section over the cabin and are joined there to the wire going to the outboard magneto.

These wires should be inspected periodically and should be replaced at the first signs of wear. Any short circuit in the ignition wires will cause the magnetoes to fail. It is therefore highly important that the ignition wires be thoroughly inspected and kept in first class condition.

STARTER SYSTEM

The starter system includes three hand inertia starters, one booster magneto, one starter crank, and three separate engine priming systems.

The engine primers are of standard type. On the outboard engine assemblies the primers project through the lower cowling and are supplied with gasoline from a small valve on the carburetor. The primer for the center engine is located on the instrument board and is supplied from a small

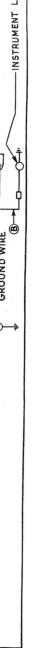

INSTRUMENT LIGHT

MAGNETOS L.H.MOTOR

LANDING LIGHTS WHEN INSTALLED UNDER FUSELAGE

SWITCH AND FUSE PANEL UNDER LEFT PILOTS SEAT

12 VOLT BATTERY UNDER LEFT PILOTS SEAT

INSTRUMENT LIGHTS COCK-PIT

RHEOSTAT INST.DIMMING

EMERGENCY MAGNETO SWITCH

MAGNETO GROUND WIRE

MAGNETOS CENTER MOTOR

CONNECTOR PANEL BELOW INST. BOARD

BOOSTER MAGNETO IN COCK-PIT

MAGNETOS R.H. MOTOR

INSTRUMENT LIGHT

MAGNETO SWITCHES ON CONTROL KNEE

RUNNING LIGHT LEFT

LANDING LIGHT LEFT

MAGNETO GROUND WIRE

IGNITION CONNECTOR PANEL WING CENTER SECTION OVER CABIN

MAGNETO GROUND WIRE

TORCHIER LIGHTS

DOME LIGHTS CABIN

CONNECTOR PANEL WING CENTER SECTION OVER CABIN

LANDING LIGHT RIGHT

RUNNING LIGHT RIGHT

TAIL LIGHT

CONNECTORS TAIL SECTION

DOME LIGHT WASH ROOM

LIGHT SWITCH WASH ROOM

COLOR CODE

| H.T.=HIGH TENSION |
| G = GREEN |
| R = RED |
| B = BLACK |

Figure 50—Wiring Diagram

valve at the gas shut-off located in the pilot's compartment. No service of the priming system is required other than occasional inspection for possible leaks.

Keep primer shut-off valves closed at all times when not priming engines, otherwise gas will flow into the cylinders and damage the engine when starting. If a plane has been standing for some time, it is advisable to turn engines over by hand about six revolutions with the switch off to be sure there is no gas in the cylinders.

THE BOOSTER MAGNETO

The booster magneto is used to assist in starting the engines when they are cold. This unit gives a very intense spark, which the engine magnetoes do not give when the engine is being turned over at cranking speed.

The booster magneto is bolted to the under side of the right seat in the pilot's compartment. It can be connected to either of the three engines through a plug and jack system located below the instrument board in the pilot's compartment.

THE GENERATOR

The generator is engine driven. It runs 1½ times crankshaft speed. It is of the constant voltage, variable current type and automatically takes care of the electrical power requirements and keeps the battery properly charged, provided the load taken from the electrical system is less than the rating of the generator.

Generators are supplied in three sizes, namely 15, 25 or 50 ampere rating. The proper size is selected to meet the different electrical load requirements.

If electric inertia starters are installed, it is necessary to include a 25-ampere generator to keep the battery properly charged. This generator will also take care of the lighting equipment. In addition to the generator there is a control box, voltmeter reading zero to 20 volts and an ammeter included in the equipment. The ammeter reads 30-0-30 amperes for the 25-ampere generator.

When performing service work on the generator always disconnect the positive lead on the battery to prevent short circuiting and damage to the equipment.

When the generator is working properly both ammeter and voltmeter indicators will be quite steady. Should the hand on the ammeter fluctuate violently and show full scale reading during flight it indicates that the voltage regulator in the control box is not working properly, and, to prevent the battery from becoming overcharged and possibly damaged, it would be necessary to turn the generator off by opening the toggle field switch located near the voltmeter and ammeter. After the trouble has been cleared up be sure to close the switch.

An instruction pamphlet containing detailed information on the generators is supplied by the manufacturers.

AMMETER AND VOLTMETER

These instruments are so constructed that internal adjustments are not necessary.

If the pointer should be found to be off the zero mark on the scale when there is no current on, the pointer can be readjusted and brought back to the zero mark by turning the small adjusting screw in the glass cover which is provided for this purpose.

If an instrument should give any trouble, it is usually because it has been accidentally burned out, in which event it would be necessary to install a new instrument.

Part VI

INSTRUMENTS—NAVIGATION AND ENGINE

INSTRUMENTS

Figure 51

1. Air speed indicator
2. Rheostat
3. Turn bank indicator
4. Primer
5. Instrument panel
6. Instrument panel light
7. Altimeter
8. Clock
9. Throttle tension adjuster
10. Control wheel
11. Mixture control tension adjuster
12. Control column
13. Rudder control pedals
14. Primer shutoff cock
15. Center engine gas control valve

16. Pilot's seats
17. Top release handle
18. Magnetic compass
19. Rheostat
20. Carburetor throttle controls
21. Instrument panel light
22. Tachometer
23. Oil temperature gauge
24. Oil pressure gauge
25. Ignition switch
26. Booster magneto plug handle
27. Emergency ignition cut off switch
28. Carburetor mixture control handles
29. Brake lever handle

AIR SPEED INDICATOR

ALL instruments, both navigation and engine, are of standard makes. Their installation and servicing are as simple and direct as general design will permit.

THE AIR SPEED INDICATOR is a sensitive differential pressure gauge. It indicates in terms of air speed at sea level, the pressure resulting from the flow of air past the pitot-static tube to which it is connected.

Figure 52

Air Speed Indicator

THE PITOT-STATIC TUBE consists of two separate tubes, one of which has an open end which receives the full impact of the moving air. The other tube is closed at its forward end and has small holes or slots some distance back from the end. These transmit to the interior of the tube the static pressure which may be more or less than the static pressure in the pilot's compartment where the indicator is located.

The readings of an air speed indicator are correct in terms of true speed only at sea level. At higher elevations the readings are less than the actual speed, due to the decreased density of the air. Since the support to be obtained from the air decreases with its density, the indication continues to be a correct measure of that support. In other words, if the stalling speed of an airplane at sea level is 45 m.p.h., it will stall at higher altitudes, at an indicated speed of 45 m.p.h. in spite of the fact that the actual speed may be much more. Related to its functioning as a support indicator, the air speed meter becomes an indicator of the fore-and-aft attitude of the airplane, when considered in conjunction with the tachometer. For a given engine speed, there is a certain air speed corresponding to level flight. If the air speed reading increases, it indicates that the airplane is descending. If the air speed reading decreases, it indicates that the airplane is climbing.

The pitot-static tube on the Ford plane is mounted on a tube ahead of the leading edge of the left wing where it will receive an undisturbed flow of air.

At the lowest point in the connection tubes, provision is made for a drain. Great care must be taken to be sure that the joints are perfectly tight.

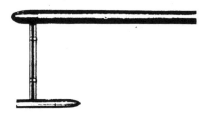

Figure 53—Pitot-Static Tube

An air speed indicator requires no service attention except the periodic removal of any water which may have accumulated in the lines.

Rubber tubing should be carefully inspected at intervals of not longer than six weeks and the tubing replaced as it deteriorates.

More air speed indicators are damaged by being blown into or sucked upon than in any other way. The pressure or suction required to secure an indication of 120 m.p.h. is only about six inches of water pressure. An ordinary person can exert a lung pressure of eighty inches of water and can suck about twice this amount. Thirty inches of pressure applied to the pitot connection, or the same suction applied to the static connection, of an air speed indicator will damage it so as to make it unfit for use. The possibilities of damaging an air speed indicator in this way are very great, unless extreme care is exercised.

Possible Causes of Trouble

Troubles with air speed indicators become apparent in three ways. First, failure of the hand to return to zero. Second, incorrect speed indication—usually too low. Third, sluggish movement of the hand and failure to respond quickly to changes in speed. The source of the trouble, in any particular case, may lie in the indicator or may be due to leaks or stoppages in the connecting tubes.

Regardless of the difficulty, the first step in locating the source of trouble is to disconnect the tube lines from the indicator. If the trouble is failure of the hand to return to zero, note if the hand comes back when the connections are removed and the instrument tapped gently. If the hand does not come to zero, the trouble is in the indicator which should be removed from the board. One of two things may be wrong: Water may have found its way into the diaphragm, or the diaphragm may have been subjected to excess pressure. Manipulate the indicator so as to let any water run out, if trapped inside. If none appears, and the hand continues to remain off zero, send the instrument to the factory for repairs.

If the hand returned to zero when the lines were disconnected the instrument is O. K. The trouble was undoubtedly due to water in the lines. Draining out the water will correct the condition.

Low readings are usually due to leaks. Sluggishness is due to stoppages in the lines. Tests for both are easily made. First, since the instrument is now disconnected, try the indicator itself for leaks, stoppage or friction. Attach a length of rubber tube to the static (S) connection. While carefully watching the hand of the air speed indicator, suck very gently on the end of the rubber tubing until the hand reaches about one-half of the full range, then close the tube by pinching or by putting your tongue over the end. The hand should stand still or return toward zero very slowly. It should not travel over 10 miles on the scale in a shorter time than 30 seconds. If the hand moves faster than this, there is a leak in the case and the instrument should be returned to the factory for repairs. If the movement of the hand is within this limit its approximate rate should be noted.

Next open the rubber tube, and note if the hand drops back quickly to zero. If it does not, there is a stoppage or excess friction in the indicator and it should be returned to the factory for repair.

Assuming that the indicator showed no leak in excess of the limit, and that the hand dropped back to zero as it should, proceed to test the tube lines for leaks and stoppages.

Connect the pitot line to the static side of the indicator (where the rubber tube has been during the previous test). Slip the rubber tube over the end of the pitot tube of the pitot-static tube. Have someone watch the dial of the indicator. Suck gently on the rubber tube, having an observer stop you when half scale is reached. Close off the rubber tube, and have observer note if the indicator hand moves toward zero and faster than when the instrument alone was tested. If so, a leak is indicated. Leaks are almost always at joints, although split tubes are occasionally found. By breaking into the line at each joint and retesting, the leak may be located by a process of elimination.

After the line has been made tight it may be tested for stoppages. Suck on the rubber tube as in testing for leaks, until the hand reaches half-scale indication. Open the tube and note if the hand drops back to zero quickly. If not, a stoppage is indicated. This may be located by breaking into the line and retesting.

The same process of testing for leaks and stoppage may be applied to the static line, but as it is impossible to make a direct connection to the static tube of the pitot-static tube, it is necessary to disconnect the line, and to attach the rubber tube directly to the disconnected tube.

Once an air speed indicator installation is made, it should last the life of the airplane without any attention beyond the occasional draining of water. If trouble does develop, its source may be quickly located if these directions are carefully followed.

TURN INDICATOR

THE TURN INDICATOR is used for controlling the flight of aircraft under conditions of poor visibility, or when for any reason it is desirable to eliminate yawing or turning. Used in conjunction with the Bank Indicator, which is built into the dial of all Turn Indicators, the pilot is able to maintain a laterally level attitude while flying straight and to bank at the proper angle when turning.

Figure 54
Turn Indicator

The sensitive element of the turn indicating mechanism is a small air-driven gyroscope, operated by the vacuum secured from a venturi tube. The gyro is mounted in such a way that it reacts only to motion about a vertical axis, being unaffected by rolling or pitching.

The gyro runs on specially designed precision ball bearings, to which oil is supplied from a reservoir within the gyro. Without any sacrifice of sensitiveness, the mechanism of the turn indicator is "damped" so that the hand cannot oscillate even under the roughest air conditions.

CARE. Every one hundred hours the jet screen should be removed and cleaned. This is located on the top of the instrument case at the rear, and is removed by unscrewing a knurled retaining unit. The Venturi tube should be inspected periodically to see that it does not become stopped up by anything blowing into it. Union nuts should be kept tight. About every three hundred hours of flying the instrument should be oiled. Oils such as "Gun oil", "Nyoil" or "Nujol" should be used for this purpose. There is but one place to be oiled. Remove the screw on the right hand side of the case. Insert six drops of oil and replace the screw.

WARNING. Do not, under any consideration, take the turn indicator apart. It is assembled at the factory by skilled instrument makers and, if damaged, should be returned to them for repairs.

TACHOMETER

The TACHOMETER indicates the speed of the airplane engine, by means of a standard flexible drive shaft.

Figure 55—Tachometer

The Tachometer should require little attention. The flexible shaft connecting the tachometer to the engine should be greased about every 250 hours. After greasing the flexible shaft, test it to see that it can easily be turned with the fingers from the engine end with the tachometer connected. If it has a tendency to turn in jerks, examine the whole shaft for sharp bends or unsupported lengths. A jerky or oscillating hand on a tachometer can usually be traced to some fault of the drive

Should the instrument at any time fail to operate, return it to the factory for repair.

ALTIMETER

The ALTIMETER, which is used to determine the height of aircraft, is simply a refined aneroid barometer, on which the dial is graduated in units of height above the ground instead of in units of pressure.

Figure 56—Altimeter

An altimeter will usually read lower than actual altitude in the summer and higher in the winter. This is due to atmospheric temperature and not to any error in the instrument.

Altimeters are also subject to errors due to changing barometric pressure during a flight. If the barometer falls, the altimeter will read high; if the barometer rises, it will read low.

Altimeters are supplied with a barometric scale, which increases their usefulness considerably. A pilot may secure information regarding the barometer reading at the field of his destination and then, on taking off, set the zero of his altimeter dial to correspond with the barometric pressure of his destination. The altimeter will then read altitudes above the field to which the pilot is headed.

An altimeter should require no care or service. Should it fail to indicate properly, the instrument should be returned to the manufacturers for repair.

CLIMB INDICATOR

The CLIMB INDICATOR shows the rate at which an airplane is climbing or descending. It does not indicate the angle of the airplane in respect to the horizontal, but is operated directly by the rate of change of atmospheric pressure which accompanies change of altitude.

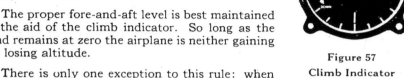

The proper fore-and-aft level is best maintained by the aid of the climb indicator. So long as the hand remains at zero the airplane is neither gaining nor losing altitude.

Figure 57

Climb Indicator

There is only one exception to this rule: when the pilot finds himself countering a strong downward current of air. The climb indicator will then show "down" and no amount of control movement will check the descent and bring the hand to zero.

Where the inability to maintain level flight is due to a strong downward air current, the movement of the air speed indicator hand, relative to that of the climb indicator hand, will apprise the pilot of the situation. Under normal conditions, a downward movement of the climb hand is promptly followed by an increased indication of air speed. If the downward movement of the climb hand coincides with a decrease in air speed indication, the pilot knows at once that he may not be able to maintain level flight and must use his climb indicator accordingly.

Construction and Operation

The climb indicator is a sensitive differential pressure gauge. It consists essentially of a metal diaphragm, one side of which is directly connected to the atmosphere, and the other side of which is connected to the atmosphere through a capillary leak tube. The diaphragm is also connected to a thermally insulated tank so that the indications of the instrument are not affected by changes in air temperature.

Atmospheric pressure varies in a known relation to altitude. This is the basis for the functioning of all barometric altimeters. As the altitude increases, the pressure decreases. This pressure decrease is transmitted instantly to one side of the diaphragm, and slowly to the other side of the diaphragm through the capillary tube. The difference in pressure between the two sides causes the diaphragm to expand or contract, and the movement is transmitted to the hand. The amount of movement of the diaphragm, and consequently that of the hand, is proportional to the rate of change of altitude.

The admission of air for actuating the climb indicator is through the connection at the rear of the case marked VENT.

The left hand connection (looking at the rear of the instrument), is made to a thermally insulated tank by means of a short length of brass tubing, both of which are part of the instrument. The right hand or vent connection is led into the pilot's compartment so that the instrument will not be disturbed by pressure fluctuations in the engine compartment. A zero adjusting screw is provided to take care of a possible shift of the zero position of the indicator hand. Should the hand of the instrument be off zero when the plane is at rest on the ground, turn this screw VERY SLOWLY until the hand returns to zero. Always watch the hand while doing this as a fraction of a turn is all that is needed in most cases to bring the hand back to zero. Tap the glass lightly with the finger while making this adjustment to overcome any possible friction. Should the instrument fail at any time to operate properly, examine the connecting tube and all connections for possible leaks. If all connections are tight and the instrument still fails to operate properly send it to the factory for repair. *Be sure* to include the *connecting tube* and *tank* with the instrument as the fault may lie in either of these, rather than in the indicator proper.

MAGNETIC COMPASS

The **MAGNETIC COMPASS** is used to indicate the direction in which a plane is headed, when flying on a straight course. It does not indicate correctly on turns which are fast enough to require an appreciable banking of the airplane. The errors increase rapidly with the increase in the banking angle, a bank of about 20° being sufficient to completely destroy the function of the compass. This condition is inherent in any compass which depends upon the earth's magnetic field for its directive effect and upon gravity for its stabilization.

Figure 58

Magnetic Compass

After being disturbed, as in a steeply banked turn, it returns to meridian quickly, and may be depended upon for an accurate indication within 30 seconds after straight flight is resumed.

In order for a compass to indicate directions accurately it is necessary that it be properly compensated. Before leaving the factory each compass is compensated after installation in the airplane.

In practically every airplane there is a magnetic field existent which causes a deviation in the true reading of a magnetic compass. By compensation we introduce another magnetic field of the same strength as that which causes the deviation and in such a direction that the compensation neutralizes the disturbance, leaving the compass free to respond to the earth's field.

The Micrometer Compensator, which is standard equipment, is completely self-contained.

To secure any required amount of magnetic force with the Micrometer Compensator, turn the screws which are exposed just between the letters E-W and N-S. The upper screw introduces magnetism for correcting the compass on East and West headings. The lower screw is used for correcting the compass on North and South headings.

To compensate a compass with the Micrometer Compensator proceed as follows:

Using a carpenter's horse or a high dolly, raise the tail of the plane to actual flying altitude. This is very important in order to secure proper results.

Determine directions by means of a magnetic compass suspended from a wing-tip, or by sighting with a surveyor's transit.

Head the airplane due North (magnetic). If compass does not read N, turn lower compensator screw until compass does read N. Use special screw-driver furnished with compass or any non-magnetic metal strip. Next head due West. If compass does not read W, turn upper compensator screw until compass does read W. Next head due South. If compass does not read S, turn lower compensator screw to take out half the error. Next head due East. If compass does not read E, turn upper compensator screw to take out half the error.

Next head the airplane successively N, 330, 300, W, 240, 210, S, 150, 120, E, 60 and 30 degrees, noting the compass indication on each heading on a Correction Chart, as shown:—

For	N	330	300	W	240	210
Steer						

and

For	S	150	120	E	60	30
Steer						

and post it in the plane within easy reach of the pilot.

The compass should require little attention beyond periodic re-checking of its compensation. Bubbles, which appear occasionally, can be easily removed as follows: Remove the compass from its bracket, with a screw driver remove filling cap. While doing this, hold compass with filling hole uppermost. Manipulate compass until bubble comes just below filling hold and drop in kerosene with a medicine dropper or fountain pen filler, until it overflows. Replace plug, screw up tightly and reinstall the compass.

It is very important that bubbles be removed from the compass, as a bubble of large size may allow the liquid to get in motion within the bowl and drag the card along with it causing the compass to spin. Do not use alcohol as it will dissolve the celluloid card and ruin the compass.

PARACHUTE FLARE

TWO PARACHUTE FLARES are mounted in the rear part of the fuselage. Their release cables run to the pilot's compartment.

The Parachute Flare, will, a few seconds after it is released, light up an area approximately a mile and a quarter in diameter from an altitude of 2,500 feet above the ground. The flare then floats slowly downward, lighting up the ground more and more brilliantly as it descends. The flare lasts for about three minutes, burning with a candle power between 300,000 and 400,000. It may be safely released at an altitude of 1,200 feet above the ground without causing any danger to life or property beneath it.

The flare consists of an illuminant and a parachute in a cylindrical sheet metal casing. At the bottom of the casing is a cap, which is retained by a spring steel band which is held in place by a releasing fork. When the releasing fork is pulled, the spring steel band flies away from the case, freeing the bottom cap and allowing the illuminant to fall out, dragging the parachute after it. At about 50 feet below the plane the parachute opens and supports the illuminant. The jerk caused by the opening of the parachute

operates a friction igniting device which in turn sets off the burning mixture.
There is no deterioration of any of the pyrotechnic material in the flare.

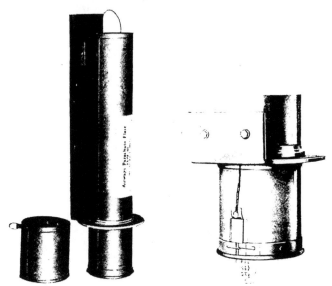

Figures 59 and 60—Parachute Flares

It is advisable when releasing a flare to have the nose of the plane
pointed slightly downward. A parachute flare should receive the following
care and attention:

The bottom of the flare which projects below the plane should be
wiped off with an oily rag at each inspection of the plane to remove any
accumulations of dirt.

About once a month the flare should be inspected as follows:

1. Insert cotter pin to "safety" the flare.
2. Release flare from its bracket and remove from the ship.
3. Work cable fore and aft to see if cable operates freely in housing. If
   cable binds, remove from casing and carefully inspect. When replacing,
   grease freely with a non-oxide grease.
4. Invert the flare, remove the cotter pin, and pull the releasing fork
   which will in turn free the spring steel band.
5. With the flare still inverted, lift out the bottom cap and clean away
   any mud or dirt accumulations. The cardboard illuminant case may
   now be pulled out an inch or less and rotated back and forth to see
   that it is free in the outer case. (Do not pull the flare out more than
   an inch, as the parachute shroud lines may be fouled or jammed when
   putting it back, thus preventing the proper release of the flare).
6. Reassemble, including "safety" pin and replace in plane.
7. Remove "safety" pin.

About once a year, the flare should be returned to the manufacturer to
have both the flare and parachute inspected.

OIL PRESSURE AND OIL TEMPERATURE GAUGES

Figure 61—Oil Pressure Gauge   Figure 62—Oil Temperature Gauge

These instruments should require no attention.   If they fail to operate properly, they should be returned to the factory for repair.

CLOCK

The clock should require no attention. Winding is accomplished by turning the knob counter clockwise. To set, pull the knob out. Should the knob appear tight when pushing it in after setting, do not force it, but turn it slightly and push again. Should the clock fail to function at any time, return it to the factory for repair.

Figure 63—Clock

Part VII

PROPELLERS

Method of Inspection

PROPELLERS

Figure 64—Propeller Assembled

ALL models of Ford Tri-motor monoplanes are equipped with forged heat-treated aluminum alloy detachable blade propellers. This type of construction possesses many advantages and a marked superiority over wooden propellers, and in addition is unaffected by climatic conditions.

Before leaving the factory all propellers are carefully checked for "track", "running" and balance. Too much care cannot be given to balancing a propeller. A metal propeller, properly balanced, should run very smoothly, insuring comfort to pilot and relative freedom from maintenance difficulties due to vibration. Not all vibration, however, can be blamed on the propeller. Faulty carburetion or poor ignition are sometimes responsible.

Once balanced, a propeller should need little attention until enough metal has been eroded or chipped away to change the weight distribution. This condition is apparent as soon as it occurs, and the remedy is obvious.

All blades are set to the correct attack or pitch for the most efficient operation under all conditions; under no circumstances should this setting be altered unless a different make of blade is substituted.

The Ford Motor Company waives all guarantees of operation and service, if the propeller blade setting on any engine is changed or tampered with.

For the guidance of operating companies who are properly equipped, the following information is given:

Assembling Propeller to Engine

In assembling the propeller on the engine shaft, it is necessary that the bore of the taper be clean and free from any dirt and also that the shaft end of the engine be free from dirt and burrs. The retaining nut should be pulled up very tight when the propeller is assembled on the engine shaft.

The best method for setting the blade angle is by the use of a protractor and a checking plate, some-

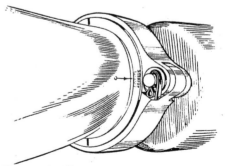

Figure 65 Close Up View of Scale on Hub

what as shown in Figure 66, and this method should be used where equipment is available. If no checking is available, the scale on the end of the hub should be used for setting the pitch.

The propeller setting is specified as the blade angle at a point 42″ from the axis.

Special Bolts for Clamping Rings

The bolts used in the clamping rings are provided with a fillet to prevent localized stress at the shoulder. These bolts are specially made from heat-treated alloy steel and should not be replaced with commercial bolts, as commercial bolts do not have the necessary strength.

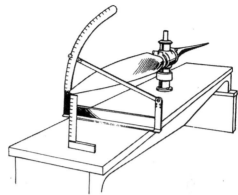

Figure 66—Protractor and Checking Plate

Straightening of Propeller Blades

Under no circumstances should welding be undertaken. The application of excessive heat will completely destroy the strength of this alloy, causing it to become weaker than aluminum. In case blades are damaged, they should be returned to the factory for repairs, because they must be annealed and re-heat treated. All repaired blades are carefully etched for hair cracks before leaving the factory.

Static Balance of the Propeller

The static balance can be checked by mounting the propeller on a mandrel passing through the hub, the mandrel being laid on suitable knife edges. The propeller should remain stationary in any position, without persistent motion. In adjusting the static balance of propellers they are first placed on knife edges with the blades in a horizontal position. If the propeller is out of balance, the light blade is removed from the hub and a small amount of heavy metal is placed into the bore of the blade end. All blades are carefully checked at the factory against a master blade, and when they leave the factory they are interchangeable as to balance. After extensive use a slight amount of wear will occur on the blades, and so, when a bent blade is replaced with a new one, there is a possibility of a slight amount of unbalance. While this never will be great enough to damage the engine or the plane, we are advocates of very accurate balancing and recommend that the blade be tried for balance on a stand whenever this is possible. The stand should be placed in a room free from air current.

Static Balance with the Blades in the Vertical Position

Perfect balance with the blades in the vertical position can be secured by adjusting the clamping rings. The eccentric weight of the bolts in these rings is sufficient to correct the unbalance, when the rings are shifted to one side. The bolt always should be moved toward the light side of the propeller until perfect balance is secured.

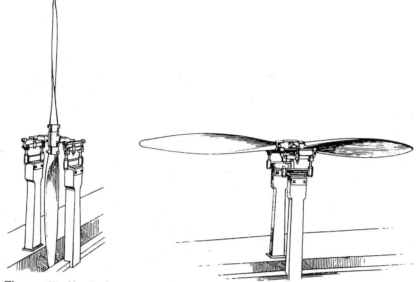

Figure 67—Vertical
Balance of Propeller

Figure 68—Horizontal Balance of Propeller

Dynamic Balance of the Propeller

The running, or dynamic, balance of the propeller is ordinarily roughly checked by testing the "track" of the propeller. The propeller is mounted on the engine or on a suitable mandrel, and the blades are swung through an arc of 180°. Both blades should pass through exactly the same path, and the amount by which they fail to do so is the "error in track."

In addition to the unbalance resulting from the centrifugal forces, it is possible also to have an unbalance due to air pressure. Thus, if the angle of one blade were set very much greater than the angle of the other, the air pressure would be greater on the blade with the higher angle, and vibration would result. The two opposite blades should be set to correspond to within 1/10 of 1°.

Care of Propeller Blades

Whenever there is any sign of pitting on the leading edge of a blade, it must be attended to immediately. If the pitting is at all bad, the rough edges should be smoothed with a fine file, the whole leading edge smoothed down with emery cloth and finished off with crocus cloth. However, the file should be avoided if possible and be used only when the pitting is so extensive as to make its use necessary. Occasionally, when severe pitting occurs, it may be necessary to remove so much material that the propeller becomes unbalanced. This condition must be watched for and be corrected.

Ordinarily, propellers are issued bright—that is, without either paint or protective coating. The best protection for the metal is a thin coat of oil, to be applied by wiping the blades with an oily cloth and this should be done after the tips have been touched up with the emery and crocus cloths to remove roughness.

METHOD OF INSPECTING
PROPELLERS

1. Etch in a 10% to 20% solution of caustic soda (1 to 2 lbs. caustic soda to 1 gallon of water), then rinse thoroughly in clean water.

2. Clean with 5% to 20% solution of nitric acid (one-half to two pints of acid to five quarts of water), then rinse thoroughly in clean water and dry.

3. Inspect for cracks and defects as follows:

   a. Examine surfaces with a magnifying glass (power 2 to 4 diameters), using special care in examining fillets and area adjacent to hub.

   b. All apparent defects should be encircled with a pencil mark and the areas rubbed with 00 sandpaper until .0005" to .002" of the surface in the immediate vicinity of the defects has been removed. Then re-etch with the caustic soda solution by applying a few drops at a time to the areas sanded, and allowing to stand several minutes. Next wipe with a cloth dampened in a water solution of nitric acid. Application of caustic soda solution should be repeated until the desired degree of etch is obtained. If the apparent defect is a crack it will appear as a distinct black line.

4. Bearing surfaces of detachable blades which fit into hubs must not be etched.

5. Propellers must be completely disassembled and all traces of paint removed before the etching process.

6. In case there is any doubt concerning the propeller clamps it is necessary to etch these clamps using the same solution and same method of inspection subsequent to the etching as is specified for the blade. It will be necessary after etching to re-cadmium plate the clamps, or to coat them with an aluminized spar varnish.

Part VIII

INSPECTION OF PLANE

Suggested Forms for
Daily and General Inspection
Special Bolts
Service Tools and Equipment

INSPECTION

The service obtained from an airplane is largely measured by the regularity and thoroughness of the inspection it receives.

For maximum safety and service the plane should receive a daily inspection covering all major points. In addition it should receive a general inspection at the end of each 25 flying hours.

Cn page 106 is shown a suggested form for a daily inspection report. Provision is made on this form for both the pilot's and mechanic's report covering the operation and condition of the plane. When making an inspection the mechanic should be constantly on the alert for anything out of the ordinary on any part of the plane.

Cn page 107 is shown a suggested general inspection form which pilots and mechanics can use in covering the 25-hour inspection. This general inspection includes a "Flight and Mechanical Report" and a "Daily Inspection and Service Record."

Inspection of the plane really starts before the pilot reaches the field. The pilot notes how the plane operates, whether or not it handles entirely satisfactorily: the performance of the engines, etc. Upon landing, he fills in his inspection report and signs it. This report gives the mechanic definite information on the operating condition of the plane. Should anything require special attention, the mechanic can go directly to that point and correct it: after which he proceeds with the regular inspection.

Cne of the first things that must be done, after the engines have cooled, to remove the engine cowling and thoroughly wash each engine. This .moves any oil or dirt accumulation and facilitates inspection by clearly showing up every part. After the cleaning operation, the engines should be carefully inspected.

Changes of oil at regular intervals as recommended in the engine instruction book are a real economy. They not only add to the life of the engine, but they add to the safety of the plane. This also applies to the oiling and greasing of the plane throughout. (See lubrication chart on page 75.)

At intervals of not more than 25 flying hours, the gasoline lines should be thoroughly cleaned. Gasoline should also be drained from the pet cock on the bottom of each tank and the strainers located on each engine should be removed and cleaned. It is also a good plan to remove the plugs from the bottom of the carburetors and drain the carburetors for a few seconds. If gasoline valves have been removed, they should be carefully checked when replaced to insure correct operation in all positions.

The successful inspector and mechanic is in reality a trouble anticipator, carefully watching for indications and conditions that might affect uninterrupted service.

After the installation of any new parts, particularly in the engine, the plane should be taken out and carefully tested before being assigned to its regular duties.

WASHING THE PLANE

Probably the best solution for washing the plane is made by placing about 12 or 15 pounds of linseed oil soap in a large pail of water and allowing it to stand about 10 to 12 hours.

The soapy solution should be applied to the entire surface of the plane. Long handle brushes are used for this purpose. The solution should not be allowed to remain on the painted surfaces longer than three or four minutes before rinsing it off. After washing the surfaces, the entire plane should be thoroughly rinsed with clean water. A hose can be used for this purpose. Two men can wash the plane in approximately $1\frac{1}{2}$ hours.

Any oil or grease on the plane can be removed with a cloth moistened in gasoline. This should be done before the washing operation is started.

The secret of clean, neat appearing planes is to wash them frequently. Not only does frequent washing add to the appearance of a plane but it considerably lessens the work involved.

When washing the upper section of the wing and fuselage, use ladders— Do not walk on top of plane.

The cabin interior may be washed with a mild soap and lukewarm water and polished with any good grade automobile or wax polish. Do not use a hose to wash interior.

DAILY INSPECTION AND SERVICE RECORD

Mfg's. No.................... Plane No.....................   Terminal................Date.................

PILOT'S FLIGHT REPORT

	L.	C.	R.		
Engine No.				Air temperature	
Oil pressure cruising				Barometer	
Oil temperature cruising				Wind velocity	
Full Throttle R. P. M.				Wind direction	
Cruising R. P. M.				Air speed—cruising	
Throttle control (Action)				Tachometer	
Altitude control (Action)				Turn & bank Ind.	
Ignition switch				Altimeter	
Carb. heater position				Compass	
Engine running condition				Clock	
Generator output				Fuel gauges	
Propeller running condition				Rate of climb	
Brakes					

REMARKS:...

....Pilot

GENERAL AIRPLANE INSPECTION

EMPENAGE	UNDER CARRIAGE	WINGS	FUSELAGE	
Stabilizer	Shock absorber	Hgr. bolts	Battery (test)	Cabin cleaned
Stb. adjustment	Struts	Ail. cont. cables	Battery switches	Windows
Fin	Fittings	Ail. hinges	Fuses	Chairs
Elevator	Axle	Ail. cont. horn	Cabin lights	Safety belts
Rudder	Wheels	Fuel tanks	Instrument lights	Toilet cleaned
Struts	Brake lining	Tank straps	Nav. lights	Starting crank
Control horns	Brake control	Fuel lines	Landing lights	Cabin heater
Hinge bearings	Brake fluid check	Fuel tank sumps	Flares	Cockpit cleaned
Control wires	Lubrication	drained	Fire extinguisher	Skin
Control pulleys	Tires	Pitot tube	Flash light	Lubrication
REMARKS:	Air pressure	Pitot tube lines	Water bottles filled	Hatch cover
	Streamlines	drained	Drinking cups supplied	Control column
		Control pulleys	Toilet paper	Rudder bar
			First aid kit	Control cables
.................Inspector			Tool kit comp.	Control pulley

ENGINE AND POWER PLANT ACCESSORIES

	L.	C.	R.		L.	C.	R.		L.	C.	R.
Engine nacelles				Oil tanks				Engine mount			
Streamlines				Oil lines				Propeller			
Valve clearance				Oil str'n'rs cl'n'd				Ex. manifold			
Rockers—greased				Fuel lines				Wiring			
Spark plugs cl'n'd				Fuel pump				Engine controls			
Breaker points				Fuel str'n'rs cl'n'd				Cowling			
Magneto oiled				Carb.str'n'rs cl'n'd				Generator oiled			
				Carb. heater							

REMARKS:...

....Mechanic

SERVICE

Gasoline put in.................Gals. | Total gasoline in.................Gals. | Plane washed.................
Oil put in.................Gals. | Total oil in.................Gals. | Engine washed L.......C.......R.......
Log book posted................. | Oil changed.................

Material, parts or instruments installed or replaced on plane on this date.................

....

....Mechanic

THIS PLANE IS READY FOR FLIGHT.

Date...

....Chief Inspector

These forms may be procured from the Ford Motor Company, Airplane Division, at small cost.

NO. 1

GENERAL INSPECTION AND SERVICE RECORD

Engines

PLANE NO._____   L_____   Date_____

                    C_____   Place_____

                    R_____

FLIGHT AND MECHANICAL REPORT

	Engine			Remarks
	L	C	R	
Fuel Pressure...........				
Oil Pressure...........				
Oil Temperature...........				
Max. R. P. M...........				
Cruise R. P. M...........				
Flying Time...........Hours...........Minutes.				Pilot...........

Chief Mechanic will check with colored pencil in square before items where special inspection or repairs are to be made.

This inspection after Trip No.........................

Total time since last serviced.......................... Last serviced at...........................

SECTION 1—Cowling	Engine		
	L	C	R
1. Engine Cowl...........			
2. Nacelle Cowl...........			
3. Removed for Inspection...........			

SECTION 3—Engine Mount	Engine		
	L	C	R
1. Cleaned...........			
2. Mount Inspected...........			
3. Nuts Tightened and Cottered			
4. Nacelle to Wing Fittings........			
5. Tubing Frame of Nacelle........			
6. Tube Formers for Cowl...........			
7. Bullett Bolts for Cowl...........			

SECTION 4—Carb. Sec. & Cont.	Engine		
	L	C	R
1. Throttle Control...........			
2. Throttle Control Clevis Pins			
3. Throttle Control Adjustment			
4. Altitude Control...........			
5. Altitude Control Clevis Pins..			
6. Altitude Control Adjustment..			
7. Alt. Cont. Packing Nut Tight			
8. Gas Strainer (cleaned)...........			
9. Gas Connections...........			
10. Hose Con. on Assembly...........			
11. Drain Cock on Strainer...........			
12. Support Fittings of Strainer....			
13. Fuel Controls...........			
14. Carb. Hold-on Nuts...........			
15. Carb. Braces...........			
16. Carb. Hot Spot...........			
17. Idling Adjustment...........			
18. Low Speed Adjustment			
19. Screen in Air Scoop.....			
20. Drain Plugs Safetied...........			
21. Oil Carb. Thtl. Shaft Bearing			
22. Primer System...........			

SECTION 2—Exhaust Ring	Engine		
	L	C	R
1. Paint Exhaust Assembly...........			
2. Ex. Ring Flex Connections.....			
3. Exhaust Ring Cyl. Flanges......			
4. Exhaust Ring Flange Gaskets			
5. Exhaust Trumpet...........			
6. Ex. Trumpet Anchor Fitting....			

SECTION 5—Gas Pump	Engine
	C
1. Gas Pump...........	
2. Release Valve...........	
3. By-Pass Valve...........	
4. Hold-On Nuts...........	
5. Gas Connections...........	

SECTION 6—Oil System	Engine		
	L	C	R
1. Oil Tank...........			
2. Oil Tank Con. on Tank...........			
3. Oil Line & Con. Tank to Pump			
4. Oil Line & Con. Pump to Tank			
5. Support Straps, Oil Tank........			
6. Support Straps, Oil Line........			
7. Oil Pump...........			
8. Oil Pump Gasket...........			
9. Oil Pump Drain Plug Safetied			
10. Oil Tank Drain Plug Safetied..			
11. Oil Sump Drain Plug Safetied			
12. Oil Screen Removed, Cleaned..			
13. Oil Pressure Line...........			

SECTION 7—Instruments	Engine		
	L	C	R
1. Oil Pressure Gauge...........			
2. Temperature Gauge...........			
3. Tachometer...........			
4. Gas Gauge...........			

NO. 2

FLIGHT AND MECHANICAL REPORT—Continued

PLANE NO._____

DATE_____

SECTION 8—Magneto Section

	Engine		
	L	C	R
	L.M. R.M.	L.M. R.M.	L.M. R.M.

1. Magneto Cleaned.. Remarks:
2. Magneto Oiled..
3. Magneto Hold-Down Bolts..
4. Connection to Spark Plugs..
5. Condition of Shielding..
6. Ground Wire Connection..
7. Distributor Blocks..
8. Breaker Points Condition..
9. Breaker Points Setting..
10. Booster Wire Connection..
11. Drive Couplings..
12. Make of Spark Plugs..
13. Gap in Spark Plugs..
14. Are Spark Plugs Tight in Cyl.?..
15. Remove and Clean All Plugs..
16. Magneto Switch..

	Engine		
SECTION 9—Starter Section	L	C	R

1. Starter Hold-On Bolts
2. Actuating Control
3. Clevis Pins for Above
4. Cover Hold-On Bolts
5. Crank Pin and Shaft
6. Support Bracket for Above
7. Check in this Space Means Remove Starter for Repairs

	Engine		
SECTION 10—Propeller Section	L	C	R

1. Number
2. Date Installed
3. Pitch of Blades
4. Condition of Blade No. 1
5. Condition of Blade No. 2
6. Clamp Bolts and Nuts
7. Hold-On Nut and Lock
8. Remove Prop. State No.
9. No. Installed
10. Reason for Removal on Back of This Report.

	Engine		
SECTION 11—Engine Section	L	C	R

1. Cylinders
2. Cylinder Hold-Down Nuts
3. Intake Pipes
4. Intake Pipe Gaskets
5. Rocker Covers
6. Rocker Cover Gaskets
7. Rocker Cover Springs
8. Valve Springs
9. Engine Cleaned

	Engine		
	L	C	R

10. Valve Adjusting Locks Tight
11. Rocker Arms Intake (greased)
12. Rocker Arms Exhaust (gsd.)
13. Clearance Exhaust Valve
14. Clearance Intake Valve
15 Push Rods Intake Greased
16. Push Rods Exhaust Greased
17. Valve Adjusting Screw (gsd.)

NOTICE—Do not open engine until oil temperature has reached 100° F. Do not run engine at full throttle on ground for more than a moment. Positively do not accelerate engine quickly.

Special work on any of the above should be noted on reverse side of report, stating section and No. in section worked on.

AIRPLANE INSPECTION REPORT

Engines

L_____

PLANE NO._____   C_____   Date_____

R_____   Place_____

SECTION 1—Wing Section

Skin_____Hatch Cover_____Baggage Compartment_____

Ailerons_____Ailerons Control Cables_____Ailerons Control Pulleys_____

Gasoline Tanks_____Gasoline Lines and Connections_____Hanger Bolts_____

SECTION 2—Fuselage

Water Bottle Filled and Cups_____Gas Gauges O. K._____Automatic Pyrene Pressure_____Booster Mag_____

Bulkhead Front_____Gas Tubing Through Bulkhead_____Skin_____

Cockpit_____Cabin Cleaned_____Seats_____Glass_____

Doors_____Pyrene_____Controls in Cockpit_____Wash Room_____Soap, Toilet Paper, First Aid Kit_____

SECTION 3—Empennage

Fin_____Attachments_____Braces_____

Stabilizer_____Attachments_____Braces_____Alignment_____Adjustment_____

Rudder_____Hinges_____Horns_____Cables_____Pulleys_____

Elevators_____Hinges_____Horns_____Cables_____Pulleys_____

SECTION 4—Tail Wheel Assembly

Wheel_____Spokes_____Tire_____Bearing Lubricated_____Shock Absorber_____Fittings_____

SECTION 5—Landing Gear Assembly

Wheels_____Spokes_____Tires_____lbs._____Struts L. H._____R. H._____

Fittings_____Streamline_____Fenders_____Shock Absorbers_____

Bearings Lubricated_____Brakes_____Pressure_____

SECTION 6—Flight Instruments

Compass_____Turn and Bank Indicator_____Altitude_____

Air Speed_____Rate of Climb_____Clock_____

SECTION 7—Service

Left Tank_____Gas, Gals._____Filled by_____

Center Tank_____Gas, Gals._____Filled by_____

Right Tank_____Gas, Gals._____Filled by_____

Right Reserve_____Gas, Gals._____Filled by_____

Left Reserve_____Gas, Gals._____Filled by_____

Right Motor_____Oil, Gals._____Filled by_____

Center Motor_____Oil, Gals._____Filled by_____

Left Motor_____Oil, Gals._____Filled by_____

Oil Drained Out by_____

Logs Posted_____Plane Washed_____

SECTION 8—Test Run by Chief Mechanic

Engine

L   C   R

Oil Pressure Idling_____

Oil Pressure Max._____

Oil Temperature_____

R. P. M. Min._____

R. P. M. Max._____

Gas Pressure_____

Final Check Made by_____   Pilot Accepting Plane_____

Date Left_____

SPECIAL BOLTS

Bolts used in vital parts of the Ford monoplane are made of special high strength steel. For replacements these bolts should be ordered from the Ford Motor Co., Airplane Division, Service Department. A list of the bolts is given below:

Ford Number	No. Req'd Per Ship	Type of Steel	Part Name	Physical Properties
AB-105-22	1	AAA	Center Engine Mount to Bulkhead bolt	
AB-106-12	1	AAA	Stabilizer Adjustment Support bolt	
AB-106-16	2	AAA	Stabilizer Brace bolt	
AB-106-33	8	AAA	Center Engine Mount to Fuselage and Bulkhead bolt	
AB-107-13	4	AAA	Outboard Engine Mount to Brace bolt	Ult. Tens. Str.—
AB-107-23	2	AAA	Outboard Engine Mount to Wing bolt, Rear	130,000 lbs. per sq. in.
AB-107-36	8	AAA	Outboard Engine Mount Brace to Wing bolt	
AB-108-20	2	AAA	Outboard Engine Mount Assembly bolt	
AB-108-22	2	AAA	Landing Gear Axle to Universal bolt	Elastic Limit—
AB-108-23	2	AAA	Outboard Engine Mount to Wing bolt, Rear	110,000 lbs.
AB-108-24	2	AAA	Landing Gear Universal Joint to Fuselage bolt	Elongation in 2"—
AB-108-41	2	AAA	Landing Gear Axle Collar bolt	15%
AB-110-23	2	AAA	Landing Gear Universal to Shock Absorber bolt	
AB-110-31	2	AAA	Outboard Engine Mount Assembly bolt	Reduction of Area—
AB-16144	2	AAA	Shock Absorber Lower Fitting bolt	50%
AB-16182	2	AAA	Outboard Engine Mount to Brace bolt	
AB-11500	12	AAA	Wing Hinge Pins	
AB-10590-1	4	AAA	Wing to Fuselage bolt	
AB-10590-2	6	AAA	Wing to Fuselage bolt	

In all other locations the standard Army and Navy AN bolt is used. These bolts have a tensile strength, min. of 125,000 lbs. per sq. in., minimum yield point of 90,000 lbs. per sq. in., elongation in 2", 15%. They are used in such locations as motor to mount bolts.

PARTS

When ordering parts, it is necessary to state the *model of the plane*, also *the plane number*. Parts are to be ordered from the Service Department, Airplane Division, Ford Motor Co., Dearborn, Mich., U. S. A.

IMPORTANT

Requests for spare parts should always be accompanied by a Purchase Order. If a rush shipment is required and the order is to be telegraphed, please mention the Purchase Order number.

RECOMMENDED SERVICE TOOLS FOR REPAIR DEPOTS

Center. Punch
Screw Driver
Gas Pliers
Long Nose Pliers
Diagonal Cutters
No. 9 Curved Snips
No. 12 Curved Snips
No. 9 Straight Snips
No. 12 Straight Snips
$\frac{1}{2}$" Cold Chisel
Rawhide Mallet
Hacksaw
Hacksaw Blades
8" Half Round File
10" Mill File
6" Round File
8" Westcott Wrench
$\frac{3}{16}$" Open End Wrench
$\frac{1}{4}$" Open End Wrench
$\frac{5}{16}$" Open End Wrench
$\frac{3}{8}$" Open End Wrench
Set Socket Wrenches
Double Socket
Hubbell Plugs

Extension Cords
Drop Light
Electric Drills
$\frac{1}{4}$" Air Hammer
$\frac{1}{8}$" Air Hammer
$\frac{3}{16}$" Air Hammer
Riveting Dollies
Ball Pein Hammer
Drift Punch
Plumb Bob
Combination Square
Goggles
6" Dividers
Paint Brushes
No. 50 Drills
No. 40 Drills
No. 35 Drills
No. 30 Drills
No. 29 Drills
$\frac{1}{8}$" Drills
$\frac{3}{16}$" Drills
$\frac{1}{4}$" Drills
$\frac{5}{16}$" Drills
Gasoline Torch
Tire Irons

EQUIPMENT FOR REPAIR DEPOTS

Air Compressors
Air Hose
Band Saw
Emery Wheel
Drill Press
Welding Outfit
Power Hack Saw
Heat Treat Pot
8' Bending Brake
3' Shear
Chain Fall

Work Bench
Bench Vise
Stock Racks
8' Ladder
6' Ladder
5'. Adjustable Horse
with 10' Adjustment
4' Horse
Miscellaneous Horses
Jack
Dollies

Book of Instruction

FORD
ALL-METAL MONOPLANE

FORD MOTOR COMPANY
DEARBORN MICHIGAN

INDEX

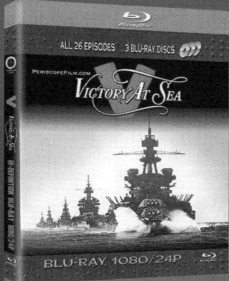

Made in the USA
Columbia, SC
03 November 2019